THE RICE
COOKBOOK

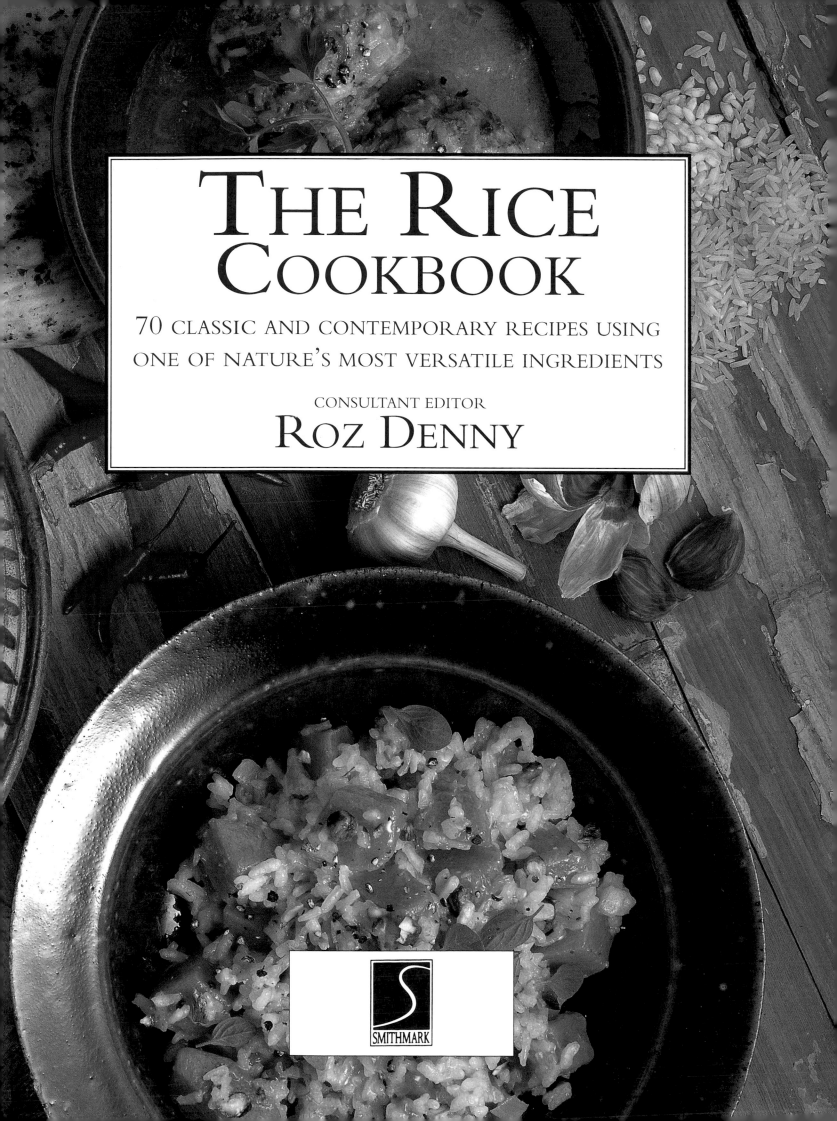

THE RICE
COOKBOOK

70 CLASSIC AND CONTEMPORARY RECIPES USING
ONE OF NATURE'S MOST VERSATILE INGREDIENTS

CONSULTANT EDITOR
ROZ DENNY

SMITHMARK

© 1996 Anness Publishing Limited

This edition published in 1996
by SMITHMARK Publishers
a division of US Media Holdings Inc.
16 East 32nd Street
New York
NY 10016
USA

SMITHMARK books are available for bulk purchase for sales
and promotion and premium use. For details write or call the
manager of special sales, SMITHMARK Publishers, a division of US Media
Holdings Inc., 16 East 32nd Street, New York, NY 10016; (212 532 6600)

ISBN 0-7651-9876-2

Publisher: Joanna Lorenz
Senior Cookery Editor: Linda Fraser
In-house Editor: Anne Hildyard
Designer: Ian Sandom
Photography: Karl Adamson, Edward Allwright, David Armstrong,
Steve Baxter, James Duncan, Patrick McLeavey, Amanda Heywood
and Michael Michaels
Styling: Madeleine Brehaut, Maria Kelly, Blake Minton and Kirsty Rawlings
Food for Photography: Carla Capalbo, Elizabeth Wolf-Cohen, Joanne Craig,
Carole Handslip, Jane Hartshorn, Wendy Lee, Annie Nichols, Jane Stevenson
and Steven Wheeler
Special photography: Janine Hosegood
Illustrator: Madeleine David

Printed in Singapore by Star Standard Industries Pte. Ltd.

CONTENTS

INTRODUCTION

Around two-thirds of the world's population is nourished every day on rice. There are thought to be about 7,000 varieties of rice grown across the globe, all with different qualities and characteristics. Rice is central to many of the world's greatest cuisines and can be used in a host of ways both savory and sweet. No other food is quite this versatile. In the West, we have just begun to appreciate the great potential of this glorious grain. Instead of relegating it to the side of our plates as an accompaniment used to mop up a little sauce or pad out the appearance of a plate, we now look on rice as the basis of a delicious meal.

The term *rice* should be applied to the milled grain only. The actual plant is known as paddy. Rice grains come from an aquatic plant that requires a great deal of water during its early growth. It was one of the first cereals to be cultivated thousands of years ago from a variety of wild grasses in many different parts of Asia. There was no one specific birthplace. The numerous varieties common today in rice-eating countries evolved according to the climate and terrain and the developing agricultural practices of the time. Even today, new strains are being developed or discovered – the latest is red rice from the Camargue in France. Rice is a very adaptable plant. Some varieties need a lot of water for growth, others can survive on less. There are grains that need constant warmth, while others can tolerate cold spells, which is why rice can be easily cultivated in so many parts of the world.

Broadly speaking, there are two main "groups" of rice that are categorized botanically into either long grain (*Oryza indica*) or short grain (*Oryza japonica*), and this determines whether the rices are long and separate, chubby and creamy or stubby and sticky. *Indica* rices have higher levels of amylose starch, which keeps them more separate after cooking. *Japonica* rices (commonly known as short- or round-grain rices) are higher in amylopectin, which gives them a more starchy quality. Needless to say, some rices fall between these two main categories, displaying aspects of both, such as Thai fragrant rices, which are long-grain and slightly sticky.

Plentiful supplies of water are important at the early growth of both types of grains. In the early dawn of civilization, this led to the need for irrigation. Controlling water supplies required great social organization if every field of paddy were to get the right amount of water. Strong social structures began to develop in rice areas, which in turn had a great effect on the cultural origins of many rice-eating civilizations. Small wonder then that rice began to play a great part in the religion and myths of these areas – unlike any other food. Legends, stories and ceremonies developed around rice. Gods and goddesses had to be humored with gifts of rice. The grains came to symbolize fertility. No other food in the world is held in such esteem or represents the soul of a people the way rice does in many parts of Asia.

This respect for rice continues on into each Asian home where rice is central to daily cooking, and great skill and techniques are handed down through generations of cooks. The very smell of rice cooking is the sign of a warm welcome for visitors to a home, and even everyday greetings include references to the eating of rice.

The main rice-growing regions of the world are China, Japan, India, Indonesia, Thailand, the southern United States and certain areas of Spain and Italy. However, many of these countries consume their own rices, so little finds its way to the West. Thailand is known as the great rice bowl of Asia,

Women harvesting the rice crop on the Indonesian island of Bali.

as it exports a lot of its crops, and the United States is also a big exporter although its home market is not as large. This obviously affects the rices we can buy in the West. Buy the best brands of rice you can afford – these will be of a better quality and won't break up during cooking, even though they may cost a few cents more.

Nowadays, the great joy of rice cooking is the incredible variety of dishes one can make, as this wonderful collection of recipes demonstrates. Nearly every major cuisine has great rice dishes, even in Europe and America. From the shaped sushi of Japan, to the pressed rice cakes of Thailand, pilaus of India, pilafs of the Middle East, risottos and paellas of the Mediterranean, creamed puddings of Portugal and Scandinavia, gâteaux au riz of France, jambalayas and gumbos of America and rice 'n' peas of the West Indies, the list is endless and the variety inspirational.

RICE AND HEALTH

For a number of years, doctors and nutritionists have been telling us that we should increase the amount of starchy foods we eat in our Western diet, and that a diet high in complex carbohydrate foods is the best for supplying us with the energy we need each day without increasing our fat intake.

Rice is an excellent starchy carbohydrate food. A generous 2-ounce portion of rice (uncooked weight), which swells to a good 6 ounces, provides us with just 170 calories and virtually no fat. It also has useful amounts of B vitamins, the minerals zinc and iron and dietary fiber and a small amount of easily digestible protein. The energy from rice is released slowly into the blood stream, it is not a quick-fix carbohydrate like sugar. In other words, it is a better-value form of energy and sustains us for longer, which is why athletes eat a lot of rice. Rice is also easily digestible,

making it an ideal first food for babies or sick and elderly people. Because it contains no gluten, rice is ideal for people who have to eat gluten-free starchy foods.

BOILING RICE

There are two easy methods of cooking rice to serve as an accompaniment. Which method you choose depends on the texture you like. But for both ways, remember to allow the rice to stand for at least 5 minutes after cooking and before fluffing with a fork to give you a better result.

Open Pan/Fast Boiling – cook rice just as you would pasta or potatoes, in a large pan of lightly salted boiling water. Boil on a medium heat for 10 to 15 minutes depending on the rice (check package instructions), then drain, rinse if preferred in hot water and allow the rice to stand in the colander for about 5 minutes before fluffing with a fork. Butter or oil can be added at this stage.

Covered Pan/Absorption – rice and a measured amount of water are simmered gently in a covered saucepan until all the water has been absorbed.

Different rices need differing amounts of water – sometimes equal quantities and sometimes as much as two-and-a-half times as much water as rice, so check the packages first. Also see the Ingredients page for more

Women sifting rice in the mountains high above the paddy fields.

guidance. After cooking, leave the pan still covered and allow to stand off the heat for 5 minutes before uncovering and fluffing as above.

RICE FOR SALADS

It is much nicer to cook rice fresh for a salad than to use leftover cold rice. After boiling (preferably using the first open pan method), rinse the rice lightly in cold running water. Drain for 5 minutes in a colander then toss lightly with vinaigrette dressing and seasoning. Then allow the rice to stand for a good 15 minutes or so before mixing in the other ingredients. This method ensures a delicious light salad in which the dressing has been absorbed into the grain instead of the type with a more cloying dressing that simply coats the outside of the grain.

REHEATING RICE

Always make sure you reheat cooked rice thoroughly for at least 5 minutes until it is piping hot, especially when stir-frying. Cooked leftover rice can be stored for about 2 days in the fridge. Rice can be frozen, but it affects the starch granules, making them seem quite chalky when reheated.

INGREDIENTS

Quality rice will have a good natural flavor which is inherent in the grain – like fine wine, it takes on the characteristics of the soil and climate where it was grown. Milling and refining can affect the flavor and texture of rice. Rice sold as "parboiled" or "easy-cook" has been heat treated with high-pressure steam. This has the effect of hardening the outside of the grain and so makes it "non-stick," but it also removes much of the natural flavor and the rice can take longer to cook and have a more chewy texture.

LONG-GRAIN RICES

These rices were originally known collectively as Patna rices (because much long-grain rice sold to Europe came from around Patna in India), but the term is little used now. A lot of the long-grain rice sold in America is of excellent quality, especially that grown around Arkansas, Texas and California. Whole-grain, or brown, long-grain rice is higher in fiber and has a slightly nutty taste. The texture though is quite chewy and it can take up to 40 minutes to cook. Both white and whole-grain rices are available in par-

Clockwise from top left: Brown rice, long-grain rice, easy-cook rice, brown basmati rice, basmati rice and American long-grain rice.

boiled or easy-cook versions. Long-grain white rices are best cooked by the open pan/fast boiling method. Allow 12 minutes for white long-grain, 15–20 minutes for easy-cook white long-grain and 30–40 minutes for whole or brown easy-cook rices.

BASMATI

The prince of rice. A highly aromatic grain that is long and elegantly thin. The name basmati means fragrant in Hindi. The scent during cooking is simply heavenly and quite unmistakable. The ideal rice for delicate pilafs and a must for Persian rice dishes too. Boil for just 10 minutes, although if cooking by the covered pan/absorption method allow only one-and-a-half cups of water to one cup of rice. Basmati rice benefits from rinsing in a bowl with plenty of cold water and a light soaking for 10 minutes before cooking. This helps lighten the grain. Brown basmati is a lighter whole-grain rice although slightly higher in fiber. It takes only 25 minutes to cook.

RISOTTO RICES

These are shorter-grained varieties with higher levels of starch.

Clockwise from top left: Three different varieties of Arborio rice, and another risotto rice, Carnaroli rice.

Clockwise from top: Ground rice, flaked rice and pudding rice.

and are used for puddings served with sugar and coconut cream. Black glutinous rice is popular in Southeast Asia for sweet dishes.

RED RICES

In the wild, rice is a light red color. Sometimes this characteristic is bred back into long-grain rices. Examples are the Wehani rice from California and more recently a semi-wild cultivated red rice from the Camargue, with a flavor slightly reminiscent of buckwheat.

WILD RICE

This is actually not a true rice at all, but a form of aquatic grass found growing around lakes in Canada and North America. The best is long, dark brown and glossy. The grains should be cooked until they burst open so releasing their natural, deliciously nutty aroma. They do take a long time to cook, up to 50 minutes, and need to be well submerged in water for most of that time. A form of smaller grain, cultivated wild rice, is more easily available and cheaper. It is sometimes sold blended with easy-cook long-grain or basmati grains.

Good risotto rice gives a nice creaminess to a dish yet still retains a bite to the grain as stock is gradually stirred into the pot. The best risotto rices are Carnaroli, Arborio and Vialone Nana. Risotto rices can be used for paellas, but the stock should be added all at once to the rice and the dish simmered without stirring. Sometimes risotto rice is sold in easy-cook form; however, this affects the creaminess of the dish.

THAI RICES

Thai fragrant or Thai jasmine are high-quality long-grain rices that have a slight stickiness to them and a delicate fragrance. They take even less time to cook than basmati and are best cooked by the covered pan/absorption method with just one-and-a-quarter times the amount of water to rice. Also, no salt is added during cooking.

GLUTINOUS RICES

These are more sticky than Thai rices. The name is misleading as rice contains

no gluten. These rices are ideal for sushi as the rice sticks together for shaping and rolling. Japanese rice is a short grain glutinous rice, easy for picking up and dipping into sauces. Glutinous rices can be black or white

Clockwise from top left: Wild rice, black glutinous rice, Japanese rice, Camargue red rice, Thai fragrant rice, white glutinous rice and long-grain and wild rice.

WEEKDAY MEALS

*Rice is the ideal pantry food.
As long as it is kept clean and dry, rice
will keep indefinitely and can be cooked
at a moment's notice. Ready in just a
few minutes when a main meal is on
order but time is short, rice forms the
basis of a satisfying and tasty dish.
Risottos, pilafs and stir-fries are natural
partners for simple fresh foods such as
bacon, shrimp, fish, chicken and ground
meat. Serve any of these dishes with
a crisp salad or steamed
green vegetables.*

Fish with Rice

This Arabic fish dish, *Sayadich,* is especially popular in Lebanon.

INGREDIENTS

Serves 4–6
juice of 1 lemon
3 tablespoons olive oil
2 pounds cod steaks
4 large onions, chopped
1 teaspoon ground cumin
2–3 saffron strands
4 cups fish stock
generous 2¼ cups basmati or other
    long-grain rice
¼ cup pine nuts, lightly toasted
salt and freshly ground black pepper
fresh parsley, to garnish

1 Blend the lemon juice and 1 tablespoon of the oil in a shallow dish. Add the fish, turning to coat thoroughly. Cover and marinate for 30 minutes.

2 Heat the remaining oil in a large saucepan and fry the onions for 5–6 minutes, stirring occasionally.

3 Drain the fish, reserving the marinade, and add to the pan. Fry for 1–2 minutes per side until lightly golden, then add the cumin, saffron strands and a little salt and pepper.

4 Pour in the fish stock and the reserved marinade, bring to a boil and then simmer for 5–10 minutes or until the fish is nearly done.

5 Transfer the fish to a plate and add the rice to the stock. Bring to a boil, reduce the heat and simmer gently for 15 minutes until nearly all the stock has been absorbed.

6 Arrange the fish on top of the rice and cover the pan. Steam over low heat for 15–20 minutes.

7 Transfer the fish to a plate, then spoon the rice onto a large flat dish and arrange the fish on top. Sprinkle with toasted pine nuts and garnish with fresh parsley.

Rice Layered with Shrimp

INGREDIENTS

Serves 4–6
2 large onions, sliced and deep-fried
1¼ cups plain yogurt
2 tablespoons tomato paste
4 tablespoons green masala paste
2 tablespoons lemon juice
1 teaspoon black cumin seeds
2-inch cinnamon stick
4 green cardamom pods
1 pound fresh jumbo shrimp, peeled
    and deveined
3 cups button mushrooms
2 cups frozen peas, thawed
generous 2¼ cups basmati rice soaked
    for 5 minutes in boiled water and
    drained
1¼ cups water
1 sachet saffron powder mixed in
    6 tablespoons milk
2 tablespoon ghee or unsalted butter
salt, to taste

1 Combine the first 9 ingredients together in a large bowl. Stir the shrimp, mushrooms and peas into the marinade and leave for about 2 hours.

2 Grease the base of a heavy pan and add the shrimp, vegetables and any marinade juices. Cover with the drained rice and smooth the surface gently until you have an even layer.

3 Pour the water all over the surface of the rice. Make random holes through the rice with the handle of a spoon and pour in the saffron milk.

4 Place a few knobs of ghee or butter on the surface and place a circular piece of foil directly on top of the rice. Cover and steam over a low heat for 45–50 minutes, until the rice is cooked Gently toss the rice, shrimp and vegetables together and serve hot.

Pumpkin and Pistachio Risotto

This elegant combination of creamy golden rice and orange pumpkin can be made as pale or as bright as you like by adjusting the quantity of saffron.

INGREDIENTS

Serves 4

5 cups vegetable stock or water
generous pinch of saffron strands
2 tablespoons olive oil
1 onion, chopped
2 garlic cloves, crushed
2 pounds pumpkin, peeled, seeded and
  cubed (³⁄₄-inch cubes)
generous 2¼ cups risotto rice
scant 1 cup dry white wine
2 tablespoons finely grated Parmesan
  cheese
¼ cup pistachios
3 tablespoons chopped fresh marjoram
  or oregano, plus extra leaves, for
  garnish
freshly grated nutmeg
salt and freshly ground black pepper

1 Bring the stock to a boil and reduce to a gentle simmer. Ladle a little of it into a small bowl. Add the saffron strands and set aside to infuse.

2 Heat the oil in a large saucepan. Add the onion and garlic and cook gently for about 5 minutes, or until softened. Add the pumpkin and rice and cook for a few more minutes, until the rice looks transparent.

3 Pour in the wine and allow it to boil hard. When it is absorbed, add a quarter of the hot stock or water and the infused saffron liquid. Stir until all the liquid has been absorbed.

4 Gradually add the stock or water, a ladleful at a time, allowing the rice to absorb the liquid before adding more, and stirring all the time. After 20–30 minutes the rice should be golden yellow, creamy and *al dente*.

5 Stir in the Parmesan cheese, cover the pan and leave the risotto to stand for 5 minutes.

6 To finish, stir in the pistachios and marjoram or oregano. Season to taste with a little salt, pepper and nutmeg and scatter a few marjoram leaves over the top.

Bacon Risotto

Smoky bacon and mushrooms add an earthy flavor to this simple risotto.

INGREDIENTS

Serves 4

2 tablespoons sunflower oil
1 large onion, chopped
½ cup diced bacon
scant 1½ cups risotto rice
1–2 garlic cloves, crushed
¼ cup dried sliced mushrooms, soaked in boiling water
generous 2 cups mixed fresh mushrooms
5 cups hot chicken stock
few sprigs fresh oregano or thyme
1 tablespoon butter
a little dry white wine
3 tablespoons chopped peeled tomatoes
8–10 black olives, pitted and quartered
salt and freshly ground black pepper

1 Heat the oil in a large, heavy pan with a lid. Gently cook the onion and bacon until the onion is tender and the bacon releases its fat.

2 Stir in the rice and garlic and cook over high heat for 2–3 minutes, until the rice is well coated.

3 Add the dried mushrooms and their liquid, the fresh mushrooms, half the stock, the oregano or thyme and seasoning. Bring gently to a boil, then reduce the heat to low. Cover tightly and leave to cool.

4 Check the liquid and, if dry, add more liquid as required until the rice is cooked, but not mushy. Just before serving, stir in the butter, white wine, tomatoes and olives and check the seasoning. Serve hot, garnished with thyme sprigs.

Risotto with Parmesan

This traditional risotto is simply flavored with Parmesan cheese and golden fried onion.

INGREDIENTS

Serves 3–4

5 cups beef, chicken or
    vegetable stock
5 tablespoons butter
1 small onion, finely chopped
scant 1½ cups risotto rice
½ cup dry white wine
⅓ cup freshly grated Parmesan
    cheese
salt and freshly ground black pepper

1 Heat the stock in a saucepan, and leave to simmer until needed.

2 In a large heavy frying pan, melt two-thirds of the butter. Stir in the onion, and cook gently until soft and golden.

3 Add the rice, mixing well to coat with butter. After 1–2 minutes, pour in the white wine. Raise the heat slightly, and cook until the wine evaporates. Add one small ladleful of the hot stock. Cook until the stock is absorbed, stirring the rice with a wooden spoon to prevent it from sticking to the pan. Add a little more stock, and stir until the rice dries out again. Continue stirring and adding the liquid a little at a time. After about 20 minutes of cooking time, taste the rice and season as necessary.

4 Continue cooking, stirring and adding the liquid until the rice is *al dente*. The total cooking time of the risotto may be from 20–35 minutes. If you run out of stock, use hot water, but do not worry if the rice is done before you have used up all the stock.

5 Remove the pan from the heat. Stir in the remaining butter and the Parmesan cheese. Taste again for seasoning. Allow the risotto to rest for 3–4 minutes before serving.

Shrimp Risotto

The soft pink of this risotto comes from the addition of a little tomato paste.

INGREDIENTS

Serves 4

12 ounces fresh shrimp in the shell
5 cups water
1 bay leaf
1–2 sprigs parsley
1 teaspoon whole black
    peppercorns
2 garlic cloves, peeled
5 tablespoons butter
2 shallots, finely chopped
scant 1½ cups risotto rice
1 tablespoon tomato paste, mixed with
    ½ cup dry white wine
salt and freshly ground black pepper

1 Place the shrimp in a large saucepan with the water, herbs, peppercorns and garlic. Bring to a boil and cook for about 4 minutes. Remove the shrimp, peel them, and return the shells to the saucepan. Boil the shells for another 10 minutes. Strain. Return the stock to the saucepan, and simmer until needed.

2 Slice the shrimp in half lengthwise, removing the dark vein along the back. Set 4 halves aside for garnish, and roughly chop the rest.

3 Heat two-thirds of the butter in a casserole. Add the shallots and cook until golden. Stir in the shrimp and cook for an additional 1–2 minutes.

4 Add the rice, mixing well to coat with butter. After 1–2 minutes pour in the tomato paste and wine mixture. Follow steps 3–5 for Risotto with Parmesan, omitting the cheese and garnishing the finished risotto with the reserved shrimp halves.

African Lamb and Vegetable Pilau

INGREDIENTS

Serves 4

For the meat curry

1 pound boneless shoulder of lamb
½ teaspoon dried thyme
½ teaspoon paprika
1 teaspoon garam masala
1 garlic clove, crushed
1½ tablespoons vegetable oil
3¾ cups lamb stock
salt and freshly ground black pepper

For the rice

2 tablespoons butter or margarine
1 onion, chopped
1 cup diced potato
1 carrot, sliced
½ red bell pepper, seeded and chopped
1 cup sliced green cabbage
1 green chili, seeded and chopped
4 tablespoons plain yogurt
½ teaspoon ground cumin
5 green cardamom pods
2 garlic cloves, crushed
scant 1½ cups basmati rice
about ¼ cup cashew nuts
salt and freshly ground black pepper

1 First make the meat curry. Place the lamb in a large bowl and add the thyme, paprika, garam masala, garlic and salt and pepper. Stir, cover, and leave in a cool place for 2–3 hours.

2 Heat the oil in a large saucepan and fry the lamb over medium heat for 5–6 minutes, until browned.

3 Add the stock, stir, then cook, covered, for 35–40 minutes. Transfer the lamb to a bowl and pour the liquid into a measuring cup, topping with water if necessary, to make 2½ cups.

4 To make the rice, melt the butter or margarine and fry the onion, potato and carrot for 5 minutes.

5 Add the red pepper, cabbage, chili, yogurt, spices, garlic and the reserved meat stock. Stir well, cover, then simmer gently for 5–10 minutes, until the cabbage has wilted.

6 Stir in the rice and lamb, cover and simmer over low heat for 20 minutes or until the rice is cooked. Sprinkle in the cashew nuts and season to taste with salt and pepper. Serve hot.

Nasi Goreng

One of the most popular and well-known Indonesian dishes, nasi goreng is a great way to use up leftover rice, chicken and meats such as pork.

INGREDIENTS

Serves 4–6

scant 1½ cups (dry-weight) basmati rice, cooked and cooled
2 eggs
2 tablespoons water
7 tablespoons vegetable oil
8 ounces pork or beef fillet
2–3 fresh red chili peppers, seeded and sliced
½-inch cube terasi (shrimp paste)
2 garlic cloves, crushed
1 onion, sliced
1 cup cooked, peeled shrimp
1½ cups chopped cooked chicken
2 tablespoons dark soy sauce or 3–4 tablespoons tomato ketchup
salt and freshly ground black pepper
celery leaves, deep-fried onions and fresh cilantro sprigs, to garnish

1 Separate the grains of the cooked and cooled rice with a fork. Cover and set aside until needed.

2 Beat the eggs with the water and season lightly with salt and pepper. With a minimum of oil, make two or three thin omelettes in a frying pan. Let cool. When cold, roll up each omelette and cut into strips. Set aside.

3 Cut the pork or beef fillet into neat strips. Finely shred one of the sliced chilies and set aside.

4 Put the terasi, with the remaining chili, the garlic and onion, in a food processor, or use a mortar and pestle, and grind to a fine paste.

5 Heat the remaining oil in a wok and fry the paste, without browning, until it gives off a rich, spicy aroma. Add the pork or beef, tossing the meat constantly, to seal in the juices. Cook for 2 minutes, stirring constantly. Add the shrimp, cook for 2 minutes and then stir in the chicken, cold rice, dark soy sauce or ketchup and season to taste. Stir constantly to keep the rice light and fluffy and prevent it from sticking.

6 Turn onto a hot serving plate and garnish with the omelette strips, celery leaves, onions, reserved shredded chili and the cilantro sprigs.

Chinese Fried Rice

INGREDIENTS

Serves 4–6

2 eggs
3 tablespoons vegetable oil
4 shallots or 1 onion, finely chopped
1 teaspoon finely chopped fresh
   ginger
1 garlic clove, crushed
8 ounces cooked shrimp, shelled and
   deveined
1–2 teaspoons chili sauce (optional)
3 green onions, green parts only,
   roughly chopped
2 cups frozen peas
8 ounces thickly sliced roast
   pork, cubed
3 tablespoons light soy sauce
scant 1½ cups (dry-weight) long-grain
   rice, cooked
salt and freshly ground black pepper

1 In a bowl, beat the eggs, and season with salt and pepper. In a large non-stick frying pan, heat 1 tablespoon of the oil. Pour in the eggs and cook until just set. Roll up the omelette, cut into thin strips and set aside.

2 Heat the remaining oil in a wok, add the shallots or onion, ginger, garlic and shrimp and cook for 1–2 minutes. Do not let the garlic burn.

3 Add the chili sauce, green onions, peas, pork and soy sauce, and stir to heat through. Add the rice and fry over medium heat for 6–8 minutes. Spoon onto a platter and garnish with the omelette strips. Season to taste.

Chicken with Garlicky Rice

Chicken wings, when cooked until really tender, have a surprising amount of meat on them, and make a very economical supper.

INGREDIENTS

Serves 4

1 large onion, chopped
2 garlic cloves, crushed
2 tablespoons sunflower oil
scant 1 cup Patna or basmati rice
1½ cups hot chicken stock
2 teaspoons finely grated lemon rind
2 tablespoons chopped fresh mixed
   herbs
8 to 12 chicken wings
¼ cup all-purpose flour
salt and freshly ground black
   pepper
cilantro sprigs, to garnish

1 Preheat the oven to 400°F. Fry the onion and garlic in the oil in a large ovenproof pan until soft and golden. Add the rice and toss until well coated in oil.

2 Stir in the stock, lemon rind and herbs and bring to a boil. Cover and cook in the center of the oven for 40–50 minutes. Stir the rice once or twice during cooking.

3 Meanwhile, pat the chicken wings dry. Season the flour and use it to coat the chicken wings thoroughly, dusting off any excess.

4 Place the chicken wings in a small roasting pan and cook in the top of the oven for 30–40 minutes, turning once, until crisp and golden.

5 Serve the rice and the chicken wings, garnished with cilantro, with a fresh tomato sauce and a selection of vegetables.

Dill and Fava Bean Meatballs

These tasty beef koftas make a delightful change from ordinary meatballs.

INGREDIENTS

Serves 4

generous ½ cup long-grain rice
1 pound lean ground beef
1½ cups flour
3 eggs, beaten
1½ cups fava beans, shelled
2 tablespoons chopped fresh dill
2 tablespoons butter or margarine
1 large onion, chopped
½ teaspoon ground turmeric
5 cups water
salt and freshly ground
  black pepper
chopped fresh parsley, to garnish
naan bread, to serve

1 Put the rice in a pan of water and boil for about 4 minutes until half-cooked. Drain and place in a bowl with the meat, flour, eggs and seasoning. Knead until well blended.

— COOK'S TIP —

If fresh fava beans are unavailable, replace them with frozen fava beans. Defrost them before use.

2 Add the shelled fava beans and dill, and knead again until the mixture is firm and pasty. Shape the mixture into large balls and set aside on a plate in a cool place.

3 Melt the butter or margarine in a large saucepan or flameproof casserole and fry the chopped onion for 3–4 minutes until golden. Stir in the turmeric, cook for 30 seconds and then add the water and bring to a boil.

4 Add the meatballs to the pan, then simmer for 45–60 minutes, until the gravy is reduced to about 1 cup. Garnish with the chopped parsley and serve with naan bread.

Green Beans, Rice and Beef

INGREDIENTS

Serves 4

2 tablespoons butter or margarine
1 large onion, chopped
1 pound stewing beef, cubed
2 garlic cloves, crushed
1 teaspoon ground cinnamon
1 teaspoon ground cumin
1 teaspoon ground turmeric
1 pound tomatoes, chopped
2 tablespoons tomato paste
1½ cups water
2½ cups green beans, trimmed
   and halved
salt and freshly ground black pepper

For the rice

scant 1½ cups basmati rice, soaked in
   salted water for 2 hours
7½ cups water
3 tablespoons melted butter
2–3 saffron strands, soaked in
   1 tablespoon boiling water
pinch of salt

1 Melt the butter or margarine in a large saucepan or flameproof casserole and fry the onion until golden. Add the beef and fry until evenly browned, then add the garlic, spices, tomatoes, tomato paste and water. Season with salt and pepper. Bring to a boil, then simmer over low heat for about 30 minutes.

2 Add the green beans and continue cooking for another 15 minutes until the meat is tender and most of the meat juices have evaporated.

3 Meanwhile, prepare the rice. Drain, then boil it in salted water for about 5 minutes. Reduce the heat and simmer very gently for 10 minutes or until it is half-cooked. Drain, and rinse the rice in warm water. Wash and dry the saucepan.

4 Heat 1 tablespoon of the melted butter in the pan and stir in about a third of the rice. Spoon half of the meat mixture over the rice, add a layer of rice, then the remaining meat and finish with another layer of rice.

5 Pour the remaining melted butter over the rice and cover the pan with a clean dish towel. Secure with the lid and then steam the rice for 30–45 minutes over low heat.

6 Take 3 tablespoons of cooked rice from the pan and mix with the saffron water. Serve the cooked rice and beef on a large dish and sprinkle the saffron rice over the top.

Yogurt Chicken and Rice

This is flavored with *zereshk*, small dried berries available at Middle Eastern stores.

Ingredients

Serves 6

3 tablespoons butter
3–3½ pounds chicken pieces
1 large onion, chopped
1 cup chicken stock
2 eggs
2 cups plain yogurt
2–3 saffron strands, dissolved in
  1 tablespoon boiling water
1 teaspoon ground cinnamon
generous 2¼ cups basmati rice,
  soaked in salted water for 2 hours
3 ounces *zereshk*
salt and freshly ground black pepper
herb salad, to serve

1 Melt two-thirds of the butter in a casserole and fry the chicken and onion for 4–5 minutes, until the onion is softened and the chicken browned.

2 Add the stock and salt and pepper, bring to a boil and then simmer for 45 minutes, or until the chicken is cooked and the stock reduced by half.

3 Skin and bone the chicken. Cut the flesh into large pieces and place in a large bowl. Reserve the stock.

4 Beat the eggs and blend with the yogurt. Add the saffron water and cinnamon and season with salt and pepper. Pour over the chicken and leave to marinate on one side for up to 2 hours.

5 Drain the rice and then boil in salted water for 5 minutes, reduce the heat and simmer very gently for 10 minutes, until half cooked. Drain and rinse in warm water.

6 Transfer the chicken from the yogurt mixture to a dish and mix half the rice into the yogurt.

7 Preheat the oven to 325°F and grease a large 4-inch-deep casserole.

8 Place the rice and yogurt mixture in the bottom of the dish, arrange the chicken pieces on top and then add the plain rice. Warm the *zereshk* and sprinkle over the top.

9 Mix the remaining butter with the chicken stock and pour over the rice. Cover tightly with foil and cook in the oven for 35–45 minutes.

10 Leave the dish to cool for a few minutes. Place on a cold, damp dish towel, which will help lift the rice from the base of the dish, then run a knife around the inside edge of the dish. Place a large flat plate over the dish and turn out. You should have a rice "cake," which can be cut into wedges. Serve hot with an herb salad.

Louisiana Rice

Eggplant and pork are featured in this highly-seasoned dish.

INGREDIENTS

Serves 4

4 tablespoons vegetable oil
1 small eggplant, diced
8 ounces ground pork
1 green bell pepper, seeded and
   chopped
2 ribs celery, chopped
1 onion, chopped
1 garlic clove, crushed
1 teaspoon cayenne pepper
1 teaspoon paprika
1 teaspoon freshly ground black pepper
½ teaspoon salt
1 teaspoon dried thyme
½ teaspoon dried oregano
2 cups chicken stock
8 ounces chicken livers, minced
scant ⅔ cup long-grain rice
1 bay leaf
3 tablespoons chopped fresh parsley
celery leaves, to garnish

1 Heat the oil in a frying pan until piping hot, then add the eggplant and stir-fry for about 5 minutes.

2 Add the pork and cook for 6–8 minutes until browned, using a wooden spoon to break up any lumps.

3 Add the green pepper, celery, onion, garlic and all the spices and herbs. Cover and cook over high heat for 5–6 minutes, stirring frequently from the base of the pan to scrape up and distribute the crispy brown bits.

4 Pour in the chicken stock and stir to remove any sediment from the base of the pan. Cover and cook for 6 minutes over a moderate heat. Stir in the chicken livers, cook for 2 minutes, then stir in the rice and add the bay leaf.

5 Reduce the heat, cover and simmer for 6–7 minutes. Turn off the heat and let stand for another 10–15 minutes, until the rice is tender. Remove the bay leaf and stir in the chopped parsley. Serve the rice hot, garnished with the celery leaves.

EASY ENTERTAINING

When a crowd is expected, but table space and budgets are tight, meals based on light, aromatic rice are sure to fit the bill. Rice is highly absorbent and so enhances many exotic flavors, from spices and herbs to Asian sauces. It keeps warm without spoiling, and all these dishes can be made ahead of time and reheated as guests arrive – ready for simple serving and eating with a fork. A good serving tip is to mound rice dishes high on large serving platters and garnish with fresh herbs, brown fried onion, strips of chili pepper or maybe wedges of lemon and lime. This looks far more attractive than spooning it into deep bowls.

Smoked Trout Pilaf

Smoked trout might seem to be an unusual partner for rice, but this is a winning combination.

INGREDIENTS

Serves 4

generous 1 cup basmati rice
3 tablespoons butter
2 onions, sliced into rings
1 garlic clove, crushed
2 bay leaves
2 whole cloves
2 green cardamom pods
2-inch cinnamon stick
1 teaspoon cumin seeds
4 smoked trout fillets, skinned
$\frac{1}{2}$ cup slivered almonds, toasted
scant $\frac{1}{2}$ cup seedless raisins
2 tablespoons chopped
  fresh parsley
mango chutney, to serve
poppadums, to serve

1 Wash the rice thoroughly in several changes of water and drain well. Set aside. Melt the butter in a large frying pan and fry the onions until well browned, stirring frequently.

2 Add the garlic, bay leaves, cloves, cardamom pods, cinnamon and cumin seeds and stir-fry for 1 minute.

3 Stir in the rice, then add 2$\frac{1}{2}$ cups boiling water. Bring to a boil. Cover the pan tightly, reduce the heat and cook very gently for 20–25 minutes, until the water has been absorbed and the rice is tender.

4 Flake the trout and add to the pan with the almonds and raisins. Fluff the rice with a fork to distribute. Cover the pan and allow the smoked trout to warm in the rice for a few minutes. Sprinkle with the parsley and serve with mango chutney and poppadums.

Seafood Paella

This is a great dish to serve at dinner parties. Bring the pan to the table and let your guests help themselves.

INGREDIENTS

Serves 4

4 tablespoons olive oil
8 ounces monkfish or cod, skinned and
  cut into chunks
3 cleaned baby squid, body cut into
  rings, tentacles chopped
1 red mullet, filleted, skinned and cut
  into chunks (optional)
1 onion, chopped
3 garlic cloves, finely chopped
1 red pepper, seeded and sliced
4 tomatoes, skinned and chopped
generous 1 cup risotto rice
scant 2 cups fish stock
$^2/_3$ cup white wine
$^1/_3$ cup frozen peas
4–5 saffron strands soaked in
  2 tablespoons hot water
4 ounces cooked peeled shrimp
8 fresh mussels in the shell, scrubbed
salt and freshly ground black pepper
1 tablespoon chopped fresh parsley,
to garnish
lemon wedges, to serve

1 Heat 2 tablespoons of the oil in a large frying pan and add the monkfish or cod, the squid and the red mullet, if using. Stir-fry for 2 minutes, then transfer the fish to a bowl with all the juices and reserve on one side.

2 Heat the remaining 2 tablespoons oil in the pan and add the onion, garlic and pepper. Fry for 6–7 minutes, stirring frequently, until softened.

3 Stir in the tomatoes and fry for 2 minutes, then add the rice, stirring to coat the grains with oil, and cook for 2–3 minutes. Pour over the fish stock and wine and add the peas and saffron water. Season well and mix.

4 Gently stir in the reserved cooked fish with all the juices, followed by the shrimp. Push the mussels into the rice. Cover and cook over low heat for about 30 minutes, or until the stock has been absorbed but the rice mixture is still relatively moist.

5 Remove from the heat, keep covered and let the paella stand for 5 minutes. Sprinkle with parsley and serve the paella with the lemon wedges.

Chicken Biryani

INGREDIENTS

Serves 4

scant 1½ cups basmati rice
½ teaspoon salt
5 whole green cardamom pods
2–3 whole cloves
2-inch cinnamon stick
3 tablespoons vegetable oil
3 onions, sliced
4 chicken breasts (6 ounces each),
   cubed
¼ teaspoon ground cloves
5 green cardamom pods, seeds ground
¼ teaspoon hot chili powder
1 teaspoon ground cumin
1 teaspoon ground coriander
½ teaspoon freshly ground black
   pepper
3 garlic cloves, chopped
1 teaspoon finely chopped fresh ginger
juice of 1 lemon
4 tomatoes, sliced
2 tablespoons chopped fresh cilantro
⅔ cup plain yogurt
4–5 saffron strands soaked in
   2 teaspoons hot milk
3 tablespoons toasted sliced almonds
   and fresh cilantro sprigs, to garnish

1 Preheat the oven to 375°F. Bring a large pan of water to a boil and add the rice, salt, whole cardamom pods, cloves and cinnamon stick. Boil for 2 minutes then drain, leaving the whole spices in the rice.

2 Heat the oil in a pan and fry the onions for 8 minutes, until softened and browned. Add the chicken, followed by all the ground spices, the garlic, ginger and lemon juice. Stir-fry for 5 minutes.

3 Transfer the chicken mixture to an ovenproof casserole and lay the tomatoes on top. Sprinkle with the cilantro, spoon on the yogurt and top with the drained rice.

4 Drizzle the saffron milk over the rice and top with about ⅔ cup of water.

5 Cover tightly and bake for 1 hour. Transfer to a warmed serving platter and remove the whole spices from the rice. Garnish with toasted almonds and cilantro sprigs and serve with plain yogurt.

Joloff Chicken and Rice

This well-known, colorful West African rice dish is always a big hit at dinner parties.

INGREDIENTS

Serves 4

2¼ pounds chicken pieces (for a total
  of 4–6 pieces)
2 garlic cloves, crushed
1 teaspoon dried thyme
2 tablespoons peanut or
  vegetable oil
1 can (14 ounces) chopped tomatoes
1 tablespoon tomato paste
1 onion, chopped
scant 2 cups chicken stock or water
2 tablespoons dried shrimp
  or crayfish, ground
1 green chili pepper, seeded and
  finely chopped
scant 1½ cups long-grain rice, washed

1 Rub the chicken with the garlic and thyme and set aside.

2 Heat the oil in a saucepan until it begins to smoke. Add the chopped tomatoes, tomato paste and onion. Cook over medium-high heat for about 15 minutes, until the tomatoes are well reduced, stirring occasionally at first and then more frequently as the tomatoes thicken.

3 Reduce the heat slightly, add the chicken pieces and stir well to coat with the sauce. Cook for 10 minutes, stirring, then add the stock, the dried shrimp and the chili pepper. Bring to a boil and simmer for 5 minutes, stirring occasionally.

4 Put the rice in a separate saucepan. Transfer 1¼ cups of the sauce to a measuring cup and fill with water to make just under 2 cups. Stir the liquid into the rice.

5 Cook, covered, until the liquid is absorbed, then place a piece of foil on top of the rice, cover the pan with a lid and simmer over low heat for 20 minutes, until the rice is cooked, adding a little more water if necessary.

6 Transfer the chicken to a warmed serving platter. Simmer the sauce until reduced by half. Pour over the chicken and serve with the rice.

Special Fried Rice

This delicious recipe combines a mixture of chicken, shrimp and vegetables with fried rice. Lettuce and a sprinkling of nuts are added for extra crunch.

INGREDIENTS

Serves 4

scant 1 cup long-grain white rice
3 tablespoons peanut oil
1 garlic clove, crushed
4 green onions, finely chopped
1 cup diced cooked chicken
1 cup cooked peeled shrimp
  (rinsed, if canned)
½ cup frozen peas
1 egg, beaten with a pinch of salt
1 cup shredded lettuce
2 tablespoons light soy sauce
pinch of sugar
salt and freshly ground black pepper
1 tablespoon chopped roasted cashew
  nuts, to garnish

1 Rinse the rice in two to three changes of warm water to wash away some of the starch. Drain well.

2 Put the rice in a saucepan, along with 1 tablespoon of the oil and 1½ cups water. Cover and bring to a boil, stir once, then cover and simmer for 12–15 minutes, until nearly all the water has been absorbed. Turn off the heat and leave, covered, to stand for 10 minutes. Fluff with a fork and set aside to cool.

3 Heat the remaining oil in a wok, add the garlic and green onions and stir-fry for 30 seconds.

4 Add the chicken, shrimp and peas and stir-fry for 1–2 minutes, then add the cooked rice and stir-fry for another 2 minutes. Pour in the egg and stir-fry until just set. Stir in the lettuce, soy sauce, sugar and seasoning. Transfer to a warmed serving bowl, sprinkle with the chopped cashew nuts and serve immediately.

Seafood Pilaf

INGREDIENTS

Serves 4

2 teaspoons olive oil
1¼ cups long-grain rice
1 teaspoon ground turmeric
1 red bell pepper, seeded
  and diced
1 small onion, finely chopped
2 zucchini, sliced
scant 2 cups button mushrooms,
  halved
1½ cups fish or chicken stock
⅔ cup dry white wine
12 ounces whitefish fillets
12 fresh mussels in the shell (or cooked
  shelled mussels)
salt and freshly ground black pepper
grated rind of 1 orange, for garnish

1 Heat the oil in a large, non-stick frying pan and fry the rice and turmeric gently for about 1 minute.

2 Add the pepper, onion, zucchini, and mushrooms. Stir in the stock and wine. Bring to a boil.

3 Reduce the heat and add the fish. Cover and simmer gently for about 15 minutes, until the rice is tender and the liquid absorbed. Stir in the mussels and heat thoroughly. Adjust the seasoning, sprinkle with the grated orange rind and serve hot.

Stuffed Spring Chickens

This dish is very popular in Lebanon and Syria. The stuffing is a delicious blend of meat, nuts and rice.

INGREDIENTS

Serves 6–8
2 chickens (2¼ pounds each)
1 tablespoon butter
plain yogurt and salad, to serve

For the stuffing
3 tablespoons oil
1 onion, chopped
1 pound ground lamb
1 cup almonds, chopped
1 cup pine nuts
scant 1½ cups (dry-weight) rice,
    cooked
salt and freshly ground black pepper

1 Preheat the oven to 350°F. Remove the giblets, if necessary, from the chickens and rinse the body cavities in cold water.

2 For the stuffing, heat the oil in a large frying pan and sauté the onion until slightly softened. Add the ground lamb and cook over medium heat for 4–8 minutes until well browned, stirring frequently. Set aside.

3 Heat a small pan over medium heat and dry-fry the almonds and pine nuts for 2–3 minutes until golden, shaking the pan frequently.

4 Mix together the meat mixture, almonds, pine nuts and cooked rice. Season with salt and pepper, and then spoon the mixture into the body cavities of the chickens. Rub the chickens all over with the butter.

5 Place the chickens in a large roasting dish, cover with foil and bake in the oven for 45–60 minutes. After about 30 minutes, remove the foil and baste the chickens with the pan juices. Continue cooking without the foil until the chickens are cooked through and the juices run clear. Serve the chickens, cut into portions, with yogurt and a salad.

Festive Rice

This Thai dish is traditionally served shaped into a cone and surrounded by a variety of accompaniments.

INGREDIENTS

Serves 8

generous 2¼ cups Thai fragrant rice
4 tablespoons vegetable oil
2 garlic cloves, crushed
2 onions, finely sliced
2-inch piece fresh turmeric, peeled and crushed
3 cups water
1 can (14 ounces) unsweetened coconut milk
1–2 lemongrass stems, bruised

For the accompaniments
omelette strips
2 fresh red chili peppers, shredded
cucumber chunks
tomato wedges
deep-fried onions
prawn crackers

1 Wash the rice in several changes of water. Drain well.

2 Heat the oil in a wok and gently fry the garlic, onions and turmeric for a few minutes, until they are softened but not browned.

3 Add the rice and stir well so that each grain is thoroughly coated. Pour in the water and coconut milk and add the lemongrass.

4 Bring to a boil, stirring well. Cover the pan and cook gently for 15–20 minutes, or until the liquid has been completely absorbed.

5 Remove the pan from the heat. Cover with a clean dish towel, put on the lid and leave to stand in a warm place for 15 minutes.

6 Remove the lemongrass, turn out onto a serving platter and garnish the dish with the accompaniments.

Seafood and Rice

INGREDIENTS

Serves 4

2 tablespoons olive oil
4 ounces bacon, rind removed, diced
1 onion, chopped
2 stalks celery, chopped
2 large garlic cloves, chopped
1 teaspoon cayenne pepper
2 bay leaves
1 teaspoon dried oregano
½ teaspoon dried thyme
4 tomatoes, peeled and chopped
⅔ cup tomato sauce
scant 1 cup long-grain rice
2 cups fish stock
6 ounces cod or haddock, skinned,
    boned and cubed
1 cup cooked peeled shrimp
salt and freshly ground black pepper
2 green onions, chopped,
    to garnish

1 Preheat the oven to 350°F. Heat the oil in a large saucepan and fry the bacon until crisp. Add the onion and celery and stir until the vegetables begin to stick to the pan.

2 Add the garlic, cayenne pepper, herbs, tomatoes and seasoning and mix well. Stir in the tomato sauce, rice and stock and bring to a boil

3 Gently stir in the fish and transfer to an ovenproof dish. Cover tightly with foil and bake for 20–30 minutes, until the rice is just tender. Stir in the shrimp and heat through. Serve topped with the green onions.

Chicken Jambalaya

INGREDIENTS

Serves 10

2 chickens (3½ pounds each)
1 pound raw smoked ham
4 tablespoons lard or bacon fat
½ cup all-purpose flour
3 onions, finely sliced
2 green bell peppers, seeded and sliced
1½ pounds tomatoes, chopped
2–3 garlic cloves, crushed
2 teaspoons chopped fresh thyme or
    1 teaspoon dried thyme
24 medium shrimp, peeled
scant 3 cups long-grain rice
4½ cups cold water
2–3 dashes Tabasco sauce
6 green onions, finely chopped
3 tablespoons chopped fresh parsley
salt and freshly ground black pepper

1 Cut each chicken into 10 pieces and season with salt and pepper. Dice the ham; discard the rind and fat.

2 In a large casserole over medium-high heat, melt the lard and brown the chicken pieces all over, setting them aside as they are done.

3 Reduce the heat, sprinkle the flour over the fat in the pan and stir until the roux is deep golden brown.

4 Return the chicken pieces to the pan, add the diced ham, onions, green peppers, tomatoes, garlic and thyme and cook, stirring regularly, for 10 minutes, then stir in the shrimp.

5 Add the rice to the pan along with the water and stir to combine. Season with salt, pepper and Tabasco sauce. Bring to a boil and cook over low heat until the rice is tender and the liquid absorbed. Add a little extra boiling water if the rice dries out before it is cooked.

6 Stir the green onions and parsley into the finished dish, reserving a little of the mixture to sprinkle over the jambalaya. Serve hot.

Vegetarian Dishes

Rice and vegetarian foods are natural partners. Many rice-eating cultures have a wealth of delicious meatless recipes. In fact, all the world's oldest vegetarian religious sects have some of the most exciting rice recipes. Nutritionally, it makes sense to serve rice with a good selection of vegetables, nuts and pulses in a meal — each individual food has differing amino acid proteins, so by combining a mixture you are completing the circle of top-class protein. It is also a great way to stay healthy and enjoy good food.

Wild Rice Rösti

Rösti is a traditional dish from Switzerland. This variation has the extra nuttiness of wild rice and a bright, simple sauce as a fresh accompaniment.

INGREDIENTS

Serves 6

¼ cup wild rice
2 pounds large potatoes
3 tablespoons walnut oil
1 teaspoon yellow mustard seeds
1 onion, coarsely grated and drained in a sieve
2 tablespoons fresh thyme leaves
salt and freshly ground black pepper

For the purée

2 cups peeled and roughly chopped carrots
rind and juice of 1 large orange

1 For the purée, place the carrots in a saucepan, cover with cold water and add 2 pieces of orange rind. Bring to a boil and cook for 10 minutes, or until the carrots are tender. Drain thoroughly and discard the rind.

2 Purée the carrots in a blender with 4 tablespoons of the orange juice. Return to the pan and reheat.

3 Place the wild rice in a clean pan and cover with water. Bring to a boil and cook for 30–40 minutes, until the rice is just starting to split, but still crunchy. Drain and put to one side.

4 Scrub the potatoes, place in a large pan and cover with cold water. Bring to a boil and cook for 10–15 minutes, until just tender. Drain well and leave to cool slightly. When the potatoes are cool, peel and coarsely grate them into a large bowl. Add the cooked wild rice and stir.

5 Heat 2 tablespoons of the walnut oil in a non-stick frying pan and add the mustard seeds. When they start to pop, add the onion and cook gently for 5 minutes, until softened. Add to the potato and rice mixture, together with the thyme, and mix thoroughly. Season to taste with salt and pepper.

6 Heat the remaining oil in the frying pan and add the potato mixture. Press down well and cook for 10 minutes, or until golden brown. Cover the pan with a plate. Flip the rösti onto the plate, then slide it back into the pan. Cook the other side for 10 minutes. Serve with the reheated carrot and orange purée.

Golden Vegetable Paella

Add some chopped fresh cilantro or flat-leaf parsley to this colorful paella for an even more vibrant contrast.

INGREDIENTS

Serves 4
pinch of saffron strands or 1 teaspoon ground turmeric
3 cups hot vegetable stock
6 tablespoons olive oil
2 large onions, sliced
3 garlic cloves, chopped
scant 1½ cups long-grain rice
⅓ cup wild rice
6 ounces pumpkin or butternut squash, chopped
6 ounces carrots, julienned
1 yellow bell pepper, seeded and thinly sliced
4 tomatoes, peeled and chopped
scant 2 cups oyster mushrooms, quartered
salt and freshly ground black pepper
strips of red, yellow and green bell pepper, to garnish

3 Cover with a lid or foil and cook very gently for about 15 minutes. (Avoid stirring unneccesarily, as this lets out the steam.) Add the carrots, yellow pepper, tomatoes, salt and black pepper, cover again and leave for 5 minutes more, or until the rice is almost tender to the bite.

1 If using saffron, place it in a small bowl with 3–4 tablespoons boiling stock. Let stand for 5 minutes. Meanwhile, heat the oil in a paella pan or large heavy skillet. Fry the onions and garlic over low heat until just soft. If using turmeric, add it to the onions and garlic in the pan.

2 Add the rices and toss for about 3 minutes, or until coated in oil. Add the stock, along with the pumpkin and the saffron liquid. Stir as it comes to a boil and reduce the heat to the lowest possible setting.

> ——— COOK'S TIP ———
>
> To peel pumpkin or butternut squash, first chop the vegetable into several manageable pieces, discarding any seeds and pith, then peel with a pantry knife or an ordinary vegetable peeler.

4 Finally, add the oyster mushrooms, check the seasoning and cook, uncovered, for just enough time to soften the mushrooms without letting the paella stick. Top with the peppers and serve as soon as possible.

Stir-fried Nutty Rice

INGREDIENTS

Serves 4

¹/₂ cucumber
2 green onions, sliced
1 garlic clove, crushed
2 carrots, thinly sliced
1 small red or yellow bell pepper,
    seeded and sliced
3 tablespoons sunflower or
    peanut oil
¹/₄ small green cabbage, shredded
4 cups cooked long-grain rice
2 tablespoons light soy sauce
1 tablespoon sesame oil
chopped fresh parsley or
    cilantro (optional)
2 cups unsalted cashew nuts, almonds
    or peanuts
salt and freshly ground black pepper

1 Halve the cucumber lengthwise and scoop out the seeds with a teaspoon. Slice the flesh diagonally, then set aside until needed.

2 In a wok or large frying pan, stir-fry the onions, garlic, carrots and pepper in the sunflower oil for about 3 minutes until they are just soft.

3 Add the cabbage and cucumber and fry for another 1–2 minutes until the leaves just begin to wilt. Mix in the rice, soy sauce, sesame oil and seasoning. Heat the mixture through, stirring and tossing all the time.

4 Add the herbs, if desired, and the nuts. Check the seasoning and serve the rice piping hot.

Wild Rice with Grilled Vegetables

INGREDIENTS

Serves 4

generous 1 cup mixed wild and long-
    grain rice
1 large eggplant, thickly sliced
1 each red, yellow and green bell
    peppers, seeded and quartered
2 red onions, sliced
generous 3 cups brown or shiitake
    mushrooms
2 small zucchini, halved lengthwise
olive oil, for brushing
2 tablespoons chopped fresh thyme

For the dressing

6 tablespoons extra-virgin
    olive oil
2 tablespoons balsamic vinegar
2 garlic cloves, crushed
salt and freshly ground black pepper

1 Put the rice in a pan of cold salted water. Bring to a boil, then reduce the heat, cover and cook gently for 30–40 minutes (or follow the package instructions), or until tender.

2 To make the dressing, stir or shake the olive oil, vinegar, garlic and seasoning in a bowl or screw-top jar until thoroughly blended. Set aside while you grill the vegetables.

3 Arrange the vegetables on a grill rack. Brush with olive oil and grill for 8–10 minutes, until tender and well browned, turning them occasionally and brushing again with oil.

4 Drain the rice and toss in half the dressing. Place in a serving dish and arrange the grilled vegetables on top. Pour over the remaining dressing and sprinkle with the chopped thyme.

Persian Rice with a Tahdeeg

Persian, or Iranian, cuisine is exotic and delicious, and the flavors are intense. A *tahdeeg* is the glorious, golden rice crust or "dig" that forms on the base of the saucepan.

INGREDIENTS

Serves 8

generous 2¼ cups basmati rice, rinsed
    thoroughly and soaked
2 garlic cloves, crushed
2 onions, 1 chopped, 1 thinly sliced
⅔ cup sunflower oil
⅔ cup green lentils, soaked
2½ cups stock
½ cup raisins
2 teaspoons ground coriander
3 tablespoons tomato paste
a few saffron strands
1 egg yolk, beaten
2 teaspoons plain yogurt
6 tablespoons butter, melted
    and strained
extra oil, for frying
salt and freshly ground black pepper

1 Drain the soaked rice, then cook it in plenty of boiling salted water for 3 minutes. Drain again.

2 In a large pan, fry the garlic and chopped onion in 2 tablespoons of the oil for 5 minutes. Add the lentils, stock, raisins, coriander, tomato paste and salt and pepper. Bring to a boil; simmer, covered, for 20 minutes.

3 Soak the saffron strands in a little hot water. Remove about ½ cup of the cooked rice and mix with the egg yolk and yogurt. Season well.

4 In a large saucepan, heat about two-thirds of the remaining oil and scatter the egg and yogurt rice evenly over the base.

5 Scatter the remaining rice into the pan, alternating it with the lentil mixture. Build up in a pyramid shape away from the sides of the pan, finishing with plain rice on top.

6 With a long wooden spoon handle, make three holes down to the base of the pan and drizzle over the butter. Bring to a high heat, then wrap the pan lid in a clean, wet dish towel and place firmly on top. When a good head of steam appears, turn the heat down to low. Cook for about 30 minutes.

7 Meanwhile, fry the sliced onion in the remaining oil until browned and crisp. Drain well and set aside.

8 Remove the rice pan from the heat, still covered, and stand it briefly in a sink of cold water for a minute or two to loosen the base. Remove the lid and mix a few spoons of the white rice with the saffron water.

9 Toss the rice and lentils together in the pan and spoon out onto a serving dish in a mound. Scatter the saffron rice on top. Break up the rice crust on the pan base and place pieces of it around the mound. Sprinkle with the fried onions and serve.

Broccoli Risotto Torte

This unusual savory cake can be served hot or cold.

INGREDIENTS

Serves 6
8 ounces broccoli, cut into very
    small florets
1 onion, chopped
2 garlic cloves, crushed
1 large yellow bell pepper, sliced
2 tablespoons olive oil
4 tablespoons butter
generous 1 cup risotto rice
½ cup dry white wine
4 cups vegetable stock
4 ounces pecorino or Parmesan cheese,
    coarsely grated
4 eggs, separated
oil, for greasing the pan
salt and freshly ground black pepper
sliced tomato and chopped parsley,
    to garnish

1 Blanch the broccoli for 3 minutes, then drain and reserve.

2 In a large saucepan, gently fry the onion, garlic and yellow bell pepper in the oil and butter for about 5 minutes until soft.

3 Stir in the rice, cook for 1 minute, then pour in the wine. Cook, stirring the mixture continuously, until the liquid is absorbed.

4 Pour in the stock and season well. Bring the rice to a boil, then lower the heat to a simmer. Cook for 20 minutes, stirring occasionally.

5 Lightly grease a 10-inch round deep cake pan and line the base of the pan with a circle of waxed paper. Set the pan aside, then preheat the oven to 350°F.

6 Stir the cheese into the rice, allow the mixture to cool for 5 minutes, then beat in the egg yolks. Add the broccoli and stir to mix.

7 Whisk the egg whites until they form soft peaks, then carefully fold them into the rice. Turn into the prepared pan and bake for about 1 hour until risen, golden brown and slightly wobbly in the center.

8 Allow the torte to cool in the tin, then chill if serving cold. Run a knife around the edge of the pan and shake out onto a serving plate. If desired, garnish the torte with some sliced tomato and chopped parsley.

Kitchiri

INGREDIENTS

Serves 4

1 cup green lentils
1 onion, chopped
1 garlic clove, crushed
4 tablespoons ghee or butter
2 tablespoons sunflower oil
generous 1 cup easy-cook basmati rice
2 teaspoons ground coriander
2 teaspoons cumin seeds
2 cloves
3 green cardamom pods
2 bay leaves
2-inch cinnamon stick
4 cups vegetable stock
2 tablespoons tomato paste
3 tablespoons chopped fresh cilantro
    or parsley
salt and freshly ground black pepper

1 Cover the lentils with boiling water and soak for 30 minutes. Drain and boil them in fresh water for 10 minutes. Drain again and set aside.

2 Fry the onion and garlic in the ghee or butter and oil in a large saucepan for 5 minutes. Add the rice, stir well to coat the grains in the fat then stir in the spices. Cook gently for 1–2 minutes.

3 Add the lentils, stock, tomato paste and seasoning. Bring to a boil, cover and simmer for 20 minutes until the stock is absorbed and the lentils and rice are just soft. Stir in the fresh cilantro or parsley and check the seasoning. Remove the cinnamon stick and bay leaves before serving.

Risotto Primavera

INGREDIENTS

Serves 4

4 cups vegetable stock
1 red onion, chopped
2 garlic cloves, crushed
2 tablespoons olive oil
2 tablespoons butter
generous 1 cup risotto rice (do
    not rinse)
3 tablespoons dry white wine
4 ounces asparagus spears or green
    beans, sliced and blanched
2 young carrots, sliced and blanched
¾ cup button mushrooms
salt and freshly ground black pepper
2 ounces grated Parmesan or pecorino
    cheese, to serve

COOK'S TIP

Pecorino, a sheep's milk cheese, is a good choice for those allergic to cow's milk.

1 It is important to follow the steps for making real risotto so that you achieve the right texture. First heat the stock in a saucepan until simmering. Next to it, in a large saucepan, sauté the onion and garlic in the oil and butter for 3 minutes.

2 Stir the rice into the onion mixture, making sure each grain is coated well in the oil, then stir in the wine. Allow the wine to evaporate, then spoon in two ladlefuls of hot stock, stirring constantly.

3 Allow this to evaporate, then add more stock and stir again. Continue like this, ladling in the stock and stirring frequently for around 20 minutes, by which time the rice grains will have swelled greatly.

4 Mix in the asparagus or beans, carrots and mushrooms, season well, and cook for 1–2 minutes more. Serve immediately in bowls with a scattering of grated cheese.

Pistachio Pilaf

Saffron and ginger are traditional spices to add to rice dishes and they are delicious when mixed with fresh pistachios.

INGREDIENTS

Serves 4

3 onions
4 tablespoons olive oil
2 garlic cloves, crushed
1-inch piece fresh ginger, grated
1 green chili pepper, chopped
2 carrots, coarsely grated
generous 1 cup basmati rice, rinsed
¼ teaspoon saffron strands, crushed
scant 2 cups vegetable stock
2-inch cinnamon stick
1 teaspoon ground coriander
¼ cup fresh pistachios
1 pound fresh leaf spinach
1 teaspoon garam masala
fresh tomato salad, to serve
salt and freshly ground black pepper

1 Roughly chop two of the onions. Heat half the oil in a large saucepan and fry the onion with half the garlic, the ginger and the chili for 5 minutes until softened.

2 Mix in the carrots and rice, cook for 1 more minute and add the saffron, stock, cinnamon and coriander. Season well. Bring to a boil, then cover and simmer gently for 10 minutes without lifting the lid.

3 Remove from the heat and let stand, uncovered, for 5 minutes. Add the pistachios and mix them in with a fork. Remove the cinnamon stick and keep the rice warm.

4 Thinly slice the third onion and fry in the remaining oil for about 3 minutes. Stir in the spinach. Cover and cook for another 2 minutes.

5 Add the garam masala. Cook for a few minutes, then drain and roughly chop the spinach.

6 Spoon the spinach around the edge of a round serving dish and pile the pilaf in the center. Serve immediately with a tomato salad.

Coulibiac

This traditional Russian dish, usually made with fish and dough, can be adapted to make a light, crisp vegetarian centerpiece using filo pastry and green lentils.

INGREDIENTS

Serves 6

1 cup green lentils, soaked for
   30 minutes
5 cups vegetable stock
2 bay leaves
2 onions, sliced
¾ cup butter, melted
1 cup basmati rice
4 tablespoons chopped fresh parsley
2 tablespoons chopped fresh dill
1 egg, beaten
3 cups mushrooms, sliced
about 8 sheets filo pastry
3 eggs, hard-cooked and sliced
salt and freshly ground black pepper

1 Drain the lentils, then simmer them in half the stock, with the bay leaves and one onion, for 25 minutes until cooked and thick. Season well and set aside to cool.

2 Gently fry the remaining onion in another pan with 2 tablespoons of the butter for 5 minutes. Stir in the rice, then the rest of the stock.

3 Season, bring to a boil, then cover and simmer for 12 minutes. Leave the rice to stand, uncovered, for 5 minutes then stir in the fresh herbs. Cool, then beat in the raw egg.

4 Fry the sliced mushrooms in 3 tablespoons of the butter for 5 minutes just until soft. Let cool.

5 Brush the inside of a large, shallow ovenproof dish with more butter. Lay the sheets of filo in it, covering the base and with enough hanging over the sides to enclose the filling. Brush the layers with butter as you work.

6 Layer the rice, lentils and mushrooms in the pastry case, repeating the layers at least once and tucking the egg in-between. Season as you layer and form an even mound.

7 Bring up the sheets of pastry over the filling, scrunching the top into attractive folds. Brush the pie all over with the rest of the melted butter and put to one side to firm up.

8 Preheat the oven to 375°F. Bake the coulibiac for about 45 minutes, or until golden and crisp. Allow to stand for 10 minutes before cutting and serving.

Caribbean Coconut Rice

This rice dish is a great favorite at West Indian family meals. Serve with slices of fried eggplant if you like.

INGREDIENTS

Serves 4

generous 1 cup easy-cook
　long-grain rice
¼ cup dried pigeon peas, soaked and
　cooked but still firm
3 cups water
¾ cup creamed coconut, chopped
1 tablespoon chopped fresh thyme
　or 1 teaspoon dried thyme
1 small onion, stuck with
　6 whole cloves
salt and freshly ground black pepper

1 Put all the ingredients into a large saucepan with the salt and pepper.

2 Bring the mixture to a boil, stirring until the coconut melts, then cover and simmer for 20 minutes.

3 Remove the lid and cook uncovered for 5 minutes to evaporate any excess liquid. Remove from the heat and stir to separate the grains. The rice should be quite dry.

Lentils and Rice

The long-grain Patna rice is a favorite in India for use in everyday cooking

INGREDIENTS

Serves 4–6

4 tablespoons ghee or
　melted butter
1 onion, finely chopped
2 garlic cloves, crushed
1-inch piece fresh ginger,
　shredded
4 green chilies, chopped
4 whole cloves
1-inch cinnamon stick
4 green cardamom pods
1 teaspoon ground turmeric
scant 1½ cups Patna rice, washed and
　soaked for 20 minutes
¾ cups split green lentils, washed and
　soaked for 20 minutes
2½ cups water
salt, to taste

1 Gently heat the ghee or butter in a large heavy saucepan with a tight-fitting lid and fry the onion, garlic, ginger, chilies, spices and salt until the onion is soft and translucent.

2 Drain the rice and lentils, add to the spice mixture and sauté for 2–3 minutes. Add the water and bring to a boil. Reduce the heat, cover, and cook for 20–25 minutes, or until all the water is absorbed.

3 Take the pan off the heat and leave to rest for 5 minutes. Just before serving, gently fluff the mixture with a large fork.

——————— COOK'S TIP ———————

Frying the spices for a few minutes before adding the rice, lentils and water allows them to sweeten and become more aromatic.

Egg Foo Yung

A great way of turning a bowl of leftover cooked rice into a meal for four, this oriental dish is tasty and full of texture.

INGREDIENTS

Serves 4

3 eggs, beaten
pinch of five-spice powder
  (optional)
3 tablespoons peanut or
  sunflower oil
4 green onions, sliced
1 garlic clove, crushed
1 small green bell pepper, seeded
  and chopped
4 ounces fresh beansprouts
3 cups cooked long-grain rice
3 tablespoons light soy sauce
1 tablespoon sesame oil
salt and freshly ground black pepper

1 Season the eggs and beat in the five-spice powder, if using. In a wok or large frying pan, heat 1 tablespoon of the oil and when quite hot, pour in the egg.

2 Cook the egg, lifting the mixture away from the sides and allowing the uncooked egg to slip underneath until the omelette is firm. Remove and slice into small strips.

3 Heat the remaining oil and stir-fry the onion, garlic, pepper and beansprouts for about 2 minutes, stirring and tossing continuously.

4 Mix in the cooked rice and heat thoroughly, stirring well. Add the soy sauce and sesame oil. Adjust the seasoning, if necessary. Add the egg strips and mix well. Serve piping hot.

Basmati and Nut Pilaf

Use whatever nuts are your favorite in this dish — even unsalted peanuts are good, although almonds, cashew nuts or pistachios are more exotic.

INGREDIENTS

Serves 4–6
generous 1 cup basmati rice
1 onion, chopped
1 garlic clove, crushed
1 large carrot, coarsely grated
1–2 tablespoons sunflower oil
1 teaspoon cumin seeds
2 teaspoons ground coriander
2 teaspoons black mustard seeds
    (optional)
4 green cardamom pods
scant 2 cups vegetable stock or water
1 bay leaf
½ cup unsalted nuts
salt and freshly ground black pepper
chopped fresh parsley or cilantro,
    to garnish

1 Wash the rice in a sieve under cold running water. If there is time, soak the rice for 30 minutes, then drain it well in a sieve.

3 Stir in the rice and spices and cook for another 1–2 minutes, so that the grains are coated in oil.

6 If the rice is cooked, there will be small steam holes in the center of the pan. Discard the bay leaf and the cardamom pods.

2 In a large shallow frying pan, gently fry the onion, garlic and carrot in the oil for 3–4 minutes.

4 Pour in the stock or water, add the bay leaf and season well. Bring to a boil, cover and simmer very gently.

5 Remove from the heat without lifting the lid. Let stand on one side for about 5 minutes.

7 Stir in the nuts and check the seasoning. Sprinkle with the chopped parsley or cilantro.

SIDE DISHES AND SNACKS

*Rice is not only for main meals. It lends
itself easily to quick light food and even
canapés. Japanese sushi is perhaps the
best-known quick rice meal – seasoned
sticky rice is shaped deftly into rolls or
molds to be served with sliced fish or
wrapped in seaweed sheets. Creamy
risotto rice is obligingly easy to form
into bite-size balls when cold, ready for
coating in crumbs and deep frying,
while long-grain rice can be rolled inside
vine leaves for the classic Greek
appetizer Dolmades. Then there is the
other great use of rice – as a tasty
accompaniment to a colorful selection of
vegetables or flavorings.*

Spicy Rice Cakes

INGREDIENTS

Makes 16 cakes

1 garlic clove, crushed
½-inch piece fresh ginger, peeled and
    finely chopped
¼ teaspoon ground turmeric
1 teaspoon sugar
½ teaspoon salt
1 teaspoon chili sauce
2 teaspoons fish sauce or soy sauce
2 tablespoons chopped fresh cilantro
juice of ½ lime
generous ½ cup (dry-weight) long-
    grain rice, cooked
peanuts, chopped
⅔ cup vegetable oil, for
    deep-frying
fresh cilantro sprigs, to garnish

1 In a food processor, process the
garlic, ginger and turmeric. Add
the sugar, salt, chili and fish sauce,
chopped cilantro and lime juice.

2 Add three-quarters of the cooked
rice and process until smooth and
sticky. Transfer to a mixing bowl and
stir in the remainder of the rice.
Wet your hands and shape into
thumb-size balls.

3 Roll the balls in chopped peanuts
to coat evenly. Then set aside until
ready to cook and serve.

4 Heat the vegetable oil in a deep-
frying pan. Prepare a tray lined
with paper towels to drain the rice
cakes. Deep-fry three cakes at a time
until crisp and golden, remove with a
slotted spoon, then drain on the paper
towels before serving hot.

Red Rice Rissoles

INGREDIENTS

Serves 6

1 large red onion, chopped
1 red pepper, chopped
2 garlic cloves, crushed
1 red chili pepper, finely chopped
2 tablespoons olive oil
2 tablespoons butter
generous 1 cup risotto rice
4 cups vegetable stock
4 sun-dried tomatoes, chopped
2 tablespoons tomato paste
2 teaspoons dried oregano
3 tablespoons chopped fresh parsley
6 ounces sharp cheese, such as
    smoked Cheddar
1 egg, beaten
1 cup dried breadcrumbs
peanut oil, for deep frying
salt and freshly ground black pepper

1 Fry the onion, pepper, garlic
and chili in the oil and butter for
5 minutes. Stir in the rice and fry for
2 minutes more.

2 Pour in the stock and add the
sun-dried tomatoes, tomato paste,
oregano and seasoning. Bring to a boil,
stirring occasionally, then cover and
simmer for 20 minutes.

3 Stir in the parsley then transfer to
a shallow dish and chill until firm.
Divide the chilled rice into 12 equal
portions and shape into balls.

4 Cut the cheese into 12 pieces and
press a nugget into the center of
each rice rissole.

5 Put the beaten egg in one bowl and
the breadcrumbs in another. Dip
the rissoles first into the egg, then into
the breadcrumbs, coating each of them
evenly.

6 Chill the rissoles for 30 minutes.
Fill a deep-frying pan one-third full
of oil and heat. Test with a cube of
day-old bread; it should turn brown in
less than a minute.

7 Fry the rissoles in batches for
3–4 minutes, reheating the oil in
between. Drain on paper towels and
keep warm, uncovered. Serve with a
side salad.

Stuffed Bell Peppers

INGREDIENTS

Serves 6

6 bell peppers (2 each red, yellow
  and green)
2 tablespoons olive oil
1 large onion, finely chopped
3–4 green onions, finely chopped
9 ounces ground lamb
2 garlic cloves, crushed (optional)
¼ cup yellow split peas
½ cup cooked long-grain rice
2 tablespoons finely chopped
  fresh parsley
2 tablespoons finely chopped fresh mint
2 tablespoons snipped fresh chives
1 teaspoon ground cinnamon
juice of 2 lemons
2 tablespoons tomato paste (optional)
1 can (14 ounces) chopped tomatoes
knob of butter
salt and freshly ground black pepper
plain yogurt and naan, to serve

1 Cut off the pepper tops and set aside. Remove the seeds and cores and trim the bases so they stand squarely. Cook in boiling salted water for 5 minutes, then drain, rinse under cold water and set aside.

2 Heat the oil in a large saucepan or flameproof casserole and fry the onion and green onions for about 4–5 minutes until golden brown. Add the lamb and fry over medium heat until well browned, stirring frequently. Stir in the garlic, if using.

3 Place the split peas in a small pan with enough water to cover, bring to a boil and then simmer gently for 12–15 minutes until soft. Drain.

4 Stir the split peas, cooked rice, herbs, cinnamon, juice of 1 lemon, and the tomato paste, if using, into the meat. Season with salt and pepper and stir until well combined.

5 Spoon the rice and split pea mixture into the peppers and place the reserved lids on top.

6 Pour the chopped tomatoes into a large saucepan or flameproof casserole and add the remaining lemon juice and butter. Arrange the peppers in the pan with the stems up. Bring to a boil, then cover tightly and cook over low heat for 40–45 minutes, until the peppers are tender.

7 Serve the peppers with the tomato sauce, yogurt and naan.

Dolmades

Dolmeh, meaning "stuffed" in Persian, generally refers to any vegetable or fruit stuffed with meat, rice and herbs. It is a favorite dish throughout the Middle East.

INGREDIENTS

Serves 4–6
9 ounces vine leaves
2 tablespoons olive oil
1 large onion, finely chopped
9 ounces minced lamb
¼ cup yellow split peas
½ cup cooked long-grain rice
2 tablespoons chopped fresh parsley
2 tablespoons chopped fresh mint
2 tablespoons snipped fresh chives
3–4 green onions, finely chopped
juice of 2 lemons
2 tablespoons tomato paste (optional)
2 tablespoons sugar
salt and freshly ground black pepper
plain yogurt and pita bread, to serve

1 If using fresh vine leaves, blanch them in boiling water for 1–2 minutes to soften. If using bottled vine leaves, rinse under cold water.

2 Heat the oil in a large frying pan and fry the onion for 3–4 minutes until slightly softened. Add the lamb and fry over medium heat until well browned, stirring frequently. Season with salt and pepper.

3 Place the split peas in a small pan with enough water to cover and bring to a boil. Cover the pan and simmer for 12–15 minutes until soft. Drain the split peas, if necessary.

4 Stir the split peas, cooked rice, chopped herbs, green onions, and the juice of one of the lemons into the meat. Add the tomato paste, if using, and then knead the mixture with your hands until thoroughly blended.

5 Flatten a vine leaf with the vein side up. Place 1 tablespoon of the meat mixture on the leaf and fold the stem end over the meat. Fold the sides in toward the center and then fold over to make a neat package. Continue until all the filling has been used.

COOK'S TIP

If using preserved vine leaves, soak them overnight in cold water and rinse several times before use.

---

6 Line the base of a large saucepan with several unstuffed leaves and arrange the rolled leaves in tight layers on top. Stir the remaining lemon juice and the sugar into about ⅔ cup water and pour over the leaves. Place a small heat-resistant plate over the Dolmades to keep them in position. Cover the pan with a tight-fitting lid and cook over a very low heat for 2 hours, checking occasionally and adding a little extra water if the pan begins to boil dry. Serve warm or cold with yogurt and warm pita bread.

Basmati and Lentil Salad

INGREDIENTS

Serves 6
1 cup Puy lentils
generous 1 cup basmati rice, rinsed
2 carrots, coarsely grated
1 cucumber, halved, seeded and
    coarsely grated
3 green onions, sliced
3 tablespoons chopped fresh parsley

For the dressing
2 tablespoons sunflower oil
2 tablespoons extra virgin olive oil
2 tablespoons white wine vinegar
2 tablespoons fresh lemon juice
generous pinch granulated sugar
salt and freshly ground black pepper

1 Soak the lentils for 30 minutes. Meanwhile, make the dressing by shaking all the ingredients together in a screw-top jar. Set aside.

2 Drain the lentils, then boil them in unsalted water for 20–25 minutes or until soft. Drain thoroughly.

3 Meanwhile boil the basmati rice in lightly salted water for 10 minutes, then drain.

4 Combine the rice and lentils with the dressing and season well. Leave to cool thoroughly.

5 Add the carrots, cucumber, onions and parsley. Spoon into a serving dish and chill before serving.

COOK'S TIP

Puy lentils from France are small, deliciously nutty pulses, highly prized by gourmets. They blend beautifully with aromatic basmati rice.

Wild Rice with Julienned Vegetables

INGREDIENTS

Serves 4
1 cup wild rice, soaked
1 red onion, sliced
2 carrots, julienned
2 stalks celery, julienned
4 tablespoons butter
1/3 cup vegetable stock or water
2 zucchini, cut in thicker sticks
salt and freshly ground black pepper
toasted sliced almonds, to garnish

1 Drain the rice, then boil in unsalted water for 15–20 minutes, until it is soft and many of the grains have burst open. Drain well.

2 In another saucepan, gently fry the onion, carrots and celery in the butter for 2 minutes, then pour in the stock and season well.

3 Bring to a boil, simmer for 2 minutes, then stir in the zucchini. Cook for 1 minute more, then mix in the rice. Reheat and serve hot, garnished with the sliced almonds.

Sushi

INGREDIENTS

Makes 8–10
Tuna sushi

3 sheets nori (paper-thin seaweed)
5 ounces very-fresh tuna fillet, cut into strips
1 teaspoon wasabi paste
6 young carrots, blanched
6 cups cooked Japanese rice

Salmon sushi

2 eggs
½ teaspoon salt
2 teaspoons sugar
5 sheets nori
6 cups cooked Japanese rice
5 ounces very-fresh salmon fillet, cut into fingers
1 teaspoon wasabi paste
½ small cucumber, cut into strips

1 To make the tuna sushi, spread half a sheet of nori onto a bamboo mat, lay strips of tuna across the full length and season with the thinned wasabi. Place a line of blanched carrot next to the tuna and roll tightly. Moisten the edge with water and seal.

2 Place a square of damp waxed paper on the bamboo mat, then spread evenly with sushi rice. Place the non-wrapped tuna along the center and wrap tightly, enclosing the nori completely. Remove the paper and cut into neat rounds with a wet knife.

3 To make the salmon sushi, make a simple flat omelette by beating together the eggs, salt and sugar. Heat a large non-stick pan, pour in the egg mixture, stir briefly and allow to set. Transfer to a clean dish towel and cool.

4 Place the nori on a bamboo mat, cover with the omelette and trim to size. Spread a layer of rice over the omelette, then lay strips of salmon across the width. Season the salmon with the thinned wasabi, then place a strip of cucumber next to the salmon. Fold the bamboo mat in half. Cut into neat rounds with a wet knife.

Fried Risotto Balls

These deep-fried balls of risotto are stuffed with mozzarella cheese. They are very popular snacks in Rome and central Italy.

INGREDIENTS

Serves 4

4 cups cooked risotto
3 eggs
1 cup mozzarella cheese,
    cut into small dice
peanut oil, for deep-frying
breadcrumbs, as required
flour, to coat

1 Allow the risotto to cool completely. (The balls are better when formed from risotto made the day before.) Beat two of the eggs, and mix them into the cold risotto.

2 Use your hands to form the rice mixture into balls the size of a large egg. If the mixture is too moist to hold its shape well, stir in a few tablespoons of the breadcrumbs. Poke a hole into the center of each ball, fill it with a few cubes of mozzarella, and close the hole again with the rice mixture.

3 Heat the oil until a small piece of bread sizzles as soon as it is dropped in (about 360°F).

4 Spread some flour on a plate. Beat the remaining egg in a shallow bowl. Sprinkle another plate with breadcrumbs. Roll the balls in the flour, then in the egg, and finally in the breadcrumbs.

5 Fry the rice balls a few at a time in the hot oil until golden and crisp. Drain on paper towels while the remaining balls are frying. Serve hot.

Indonesian Coconut Rice

This is a very popular way of cooking rice throughout the whole of Southeast Asia, and goes particularly well with fish, chicken and pork.

INGREDIENTS

Serves 4–6
scant 1½ cups Thai fragrant rice
1 can (14 ounces) unsweetened
  coconut milk
1¼ cups water
½ teaspoon ground coriander
2-inch cinnamon stick
1 lemongrass stalk, bruised
1 bay leaf (optional)
salt
deep-fried onions, to garnish

1 Wash the rice in several changes of water and then put in a pan with the coconut milk, water, coriander, cinnamon stick, lemongrass, bay leaf, if using, and salt. Bring to a boil, stirring to prevent the rice from settling on the base of the pan. Cover and cook over low heat for 12–15 minutes, or until all the liquid has been absorbed.

2 Fluff the rice through carefully and remove the cinnamon, lemongrass and bay leaf. Cover the pan with a tight-fitting lid and then cook gently over the lowest possible heat for another 3–5 minutes.

3 Pile the rice onto a warm serving dish and serve garnished with the crisp deep-fried onions.

Spinach and Rice

A thick layer of spinach makes a lovely topping for this rice dish.

INGREDIENTS

Serves 4
3 tablespoons butter or margarine
1 onion, finely chopped
2 tomatoes, chopped
generous 2¼ cups basmati rice,
well rinsed
2 garlic cloves, crushed
2½ cups vegetable stock or water
12 ounces fresh spinach, shredded
salt and freshly ground black pepper
2 tomatoes, sliced, to garnish

1 Melt 2 tablespoons of the butter or margarine in a large saucepan and fry the onion for a few minutes until soft. Stir in the tomatoes.

2 Add the rice and garlic, cook for 5 minutes, then gradually add the stock, stirring constantly. Season well.

3 Cover the pan and simmer the rice for 10–15 minutes until it is almost cooked, then reduce the heat to low.

4 Spread the spinach in a thick layer over the rice. Cover the pan and cook over low heat for 5–8 minutes until the spinach has wilted. Dot the remaining butter over the top and then serve, garnished with sliced tomatoes.

Lemon and Herb Risotto Cake

This unusual rice dish can also be served as a main course with salad. It is good served cold, and packs well for picnics.

INGREDIENTS

Serves 4

1 small leek, thinly sliced
2½ cups chicken stock
generous 1 cup risotto or short-grain pudding rice
finely grated rind of 1 lemon
2 tablespoons snipped fresh chives
2 tablespoons chopped fresh parsley
¼ cup grated mozzarella cheese
salt and freshly ground black pepper
parsley sprigs, to garnish
lemon wedges, to garnish

1 Preheat the oven to 400°F. Lightly oil an 8-inch round, loose-based cake pan.

2 Cook the leek in a large saucepan with 3 tablespoons stock, stirring over medium heat, to soften. Add the rice and the remaining stock.

3 Bring to a boil. Cover the pan and simmer gently, stirring occasionally, for about 20 minutes, or until all the liquid is absorbed.

4 Stir in the lemon rind, herbs, cheese and seasoning. Spoon into the pan, cover with foil and bake for 30–35 minutes or until lightly browned. Unmold and serve in slices, garnished with parsley and lemon wedges.

COOK'S TIP

Lightly simmering vegetables in stock instead of sautéeing in oil or butter helps to cut down on fat.

Saffron Rice with Cardamom

Aromatic green cardamom pods, cloves and saffron give this dish a delicate flavor and color.

INGREDIENTS

Serves 6
generous 2¼ cups basmati rice, well rinsed
3 cups water
3 green cardamom pods
2 cloves
1 teaspoon salt
½ teaspoon crushed saffron strands
3 tablespoons low-fat milk

1 Wash and drain the rice at least twice and place it in a large saucepan with the water.

2 Toss the whole spices into the saucepan along with the salt. Bring to a boil, cover and simmer gently for about 10 minutes.

3 Test the rice and, when cooked, drain it through a sieve. Meanwhile, place the saffron and milk in a small saucepan and heat gently.

4 Return the rice to the pan and pour the saffron milk over the top. Cover with a tight-fitting lid and cook over medium heat for 7–10 minutes.

5 Remove the saucepan from the heat and leave the rice to stand for 5 minutes before serving.

Rice with Dill and Fava Beans

This is a favorite rice dish in Iran, where it is called Baghali Polo.

INGREDIENTS

Serves 4

scant 1½ cups basmati rice, soaked in salted water for 3 hours
3 tablespoons melted butter
1½ cups shelled fava beans, fresh or frozen
6 tablespoons finely chopped fresh dill
1 teaspoon ground cinnamon
1 teaspoon ground cumin
2–3 saffron strands, soaked in 1 tablespoon boiling water
salt

1 Drain the rice and then boil it in fresh salted water for 5 minutes. Reduce the heat and simmer very gently for 10 minutes. Drain and rinse in warm water.

2 Put 1 tablespoon of the butter in a non-stick saucepan and add enough rice to cover the base. Add a quarter of the beans and a little dill.

3 Add another layer of rice, then a layer of beans and dill and continue layering until all the beans and dill are used up, finishing with a layer of rice. Cook over low heat for 10 minutes.

4 Pour the remaining melted butter over the rice. Sprinkle with the cinnamon and cumin. Cover the pan with a clean dish towel and secure with a tight-fitting lid, lifting the corners of the cloth back over the lid. Steam over low heat for 30–45 minutes.

5 Mix 3 tablespoons of the rice with the saffron water. Spoon the remaining rice onto a large serving plate and sprinkle with the saffron-flavored rice to decorate. Serve with either a lamb or chicken dish.

COOK'S TIP

Saffron may seem expensive, however you need only a little to add flavor and color to a variety of savory and sweet dishes. And, as long as it is kept dry and dark, it never goes stale.

Sweet and Sour Rice

This popular Middle Eastern dish is flavored with fruit and spices and is commonly served with chicken.

INGREDIENTS

Serves 4

2 ounces *zereshk*
3 tablespoons melted butter
¼ cup raisins
2 tablespoons sugar
1 teaspoon ground cinnamon
1 teaspoon ground cumin
scant 1½ cups basmati rice, soaked in salted water for 2 hours
2–3 saffron strands, soaked in 1 tablespoon boiling water
pinch of salt

1 Thoroughly wash the *zereshk* in cold water at least 4–5 times to rinse off any grit.

2 Heat 1 tablespoon of the butter in a small frying pan and stir-fry the raisins for 1–2 minutes.

3 Add the *zereshk*, fry for a few seconds, and then add the sugar, and half the cinnamon and cumin. Cook briefly and then set aside.

4 Drain the rice, then boil in salted water for 5 minutes. Reduce the heat and simmer for 10 minutes until the rice is half-cooked.

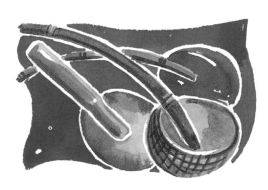

5 Drain and rinse the rice well in warm water and wash and dry the pan. Heat half the remaining butter in the pan, add 1 tablespoon water and stir in half of the cooked rice. Sprinkle with half the raisin and *zereshk* mixture and top with all but 3 tablespoons of the rice. Sprinkle over the remaining raisin mixture.

6 Blend the reserved rice with the remaining cinnamon and cumin and sprinkle it over the rice mixture. Drizzle with the remaining butter, then cover the pan with a clean dish towel and secure with a tight-fitting lid, lifting the corners of the cloth back over the lid. Steam the rice over very low heat for about 30–40 minutes.

7 Just before serving, combine 3 tablespoons of the rice with the saffron water. Spoon the rice onto a large flat serving dish and scatter the saffron rice over the top to decorate.

Thai Rice

This is a lovely, soft, fluffy rice dish, perfumed with fresh lemongrass and limes.

INGREDIENTS

Serves 4

1 stalk lemongrass
2 limes
generous 1 cup brown basmati rice
1 tablespoon olive oil
1 onion, chopped
1-inch piece fresh ginger, peeled and finely chopped
1½ teaspoons coriander seeds
1½ teaspoons cumin seeds
3 cups vegetable stock
4 tablespoons chopped fresh cilantro
lime wedges, to serve

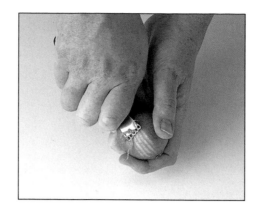

1 Finely chop the lemongrass. Then remove the zest from the limes using a zester or a fine grater.

2 Rinse the rice in plenty of cold water until the water runs clear. Drain through a sieve.

3 Heat the oil and add the onion, ginger, spices, lemongrass and lime zest and cook for 2–3 minutes.

4 Add the drained rice and cook for 1 minute, then add the stock and bring to a boil. Reduce the heat to very low and cover the pan. Cook gently for 30 minutes then check the rice. If it is still crunchy, cover the pan and leave for another 3–5 minutes. Remove from the heat.

5 Stir in the fresh cilantro, fluff the grains, cover and leave for 10 minutes. Serve with lime wedges.

Rice and Peas

This sweet and spicy dish has its origins in the Caribbean, where coconut is a popular ingredient in savory dishes.

INGREDIENTS

Serves 6
1 cup dried red kidney beans
2 fresh thyme sprigs
2 ounces creamed coconut
2 bay leaves
1 onion, finely chopped
2 garlic cloves, crushed
1/2 teaspoon ground allspice
1/2 cup chopped red or green bell
 pepper
generous 2¼ cups long-grain rice
salt and freshly ground black pepper

1 Place the red kidney beans in a large bowl. Cover with water and let soak overnight.

COOK'S TIP

Dried red kidney beans must be initially boiled vigorously for 15 minutes before lowering the heat and cooking them until tender. This ensures that natural toxins present in the beans are eliminated.

2 Drain the beans, place in a large pan and add enough water to cover by about 1 inch. Bring to a boil and boil vigorously over high heat for 15 minutes. Drain, add fresh water, and simmer for about 1½ hours, or until the beans are tender.

3 Add the thyme, creamed coconut, bay leaves, onion, garlic, allspice, red or green pepper and seasoning and stir in 2½ cups water.

4 Bring to a boil and add the rice. Stir well, reduce the heat and simmer, covered, for 25–30 minutes, until all the liquid is absorbed. Serve as an accompaniment to fish, meat or vegetarian dishes.

Tomato Rice

This delicious dish can also be served as a vegetarian main course.

INGREDIENTS

Serves 4
2 tablespoons corn oil
½ teaspoon onion seeds (optional)
1 onion, sliced
2 tomatoes, sliced
1 orange or yellow bell pepper, sliced
1 teaspoon minced fresh ginger
1 teaspoon minced garlic
1 teaspoon chili powder
2 tablespoons chopped fresh cilantro
1 potato, diced
1½ teaspoons salt
½ cup frozen peas
2 cups basmati rice, washed
3 cups water

1 Heat the oil and fry the onion seeds, if using, for about 30 seconds. Add the sliced onion and fry for about 5 minutes.

2 Gradually add the sliced tomatoes and bell pepper, ginger, garlic, chili powder, cilantro, potato, salt and peas and stir-fry over medium heat for 5 minutes more.

3 Add the rice and stir for about 1 minute until well coated.

4 Pour in the water and bring the rice to a boil, then lower the heat to medium. Cover and cook for 12–15 minutes. Leave the rice to stand for 5 minutes and then serve.

Pea and Mushroom Pilau

It is best to use button mushrooms and petit pois for this delectable rice dish.

INGREDIENTS

Serves 6
2¼ cups basmati rice
2 tablespoons vegetable oil
½ teaspoon black cumin seeds
2 black cardamom pods
2-inch cinnamon stick
3 garlic cloves, sliced
1 teaspoon salt
1 tomato, sliced
¾ cup button mushrooms, trimmed
1 cup petit pois
3 cups water

1 Wash the rice at least twice and set aside in a sieve to drain thoroughly.

2 In a medium saucepan, heat the oil and add the spices, garlic and salt.

3 Add the tomato and mushrooms and stir-fry the mixture over medium-high heat for 2–3 minutes.

4 Add the drained rice and peas and stir gently, taking care not to break the rice.

5 Add the water and bring to a boil. Lower the heat, cover and continue to cook for 15–20 minutes.

Tanzanian Vegetable Rice

Serve this tasty dish as an accompaniment to baked chicken or fish. Add the vegetables near the end of cooking so that they remain crisp.

INGREDIENTS

Serves 4
scant 1½ cups basmati rice
3 tablespoons vegetable oil
1 onion, chopped
2 garlic cloves, crushed
3 cups vegetable stock or water
1 cup corn
½ red or green bell pepper, chopped
1 large carrot, grated

1 Wash the rice in a sieve under cold water, then leave to drain thoroughly for about 15 minutes.

2 Heat the oil in a large saucepan and fry the onion for a few minutes over medium heat until it just becomes soft.

3 Add the rice and stir-fry for about 10 minutes, taking care to stir constantly so that the rice doesn't stick to the pan.

4 Add the garlic and the stock or water and stir well. Bring to a boil and cook over a high heat for 5 minutes, then reduce the heat, cover and cook for 20 minutes.

5 Scatter the corn over the rice, then spread the pepper on top and sprinkle over the grated carrot.

6 Cover the saucepan tightly and steam over low heat until the rice is cooked, then mix together with a fork and serve immediately.

Rice with Seeds and Spices

This dish provides a change from plain boiled rice, and is a colorful accompaniment to serve with curries or grilled meats.

INGREDIENTS

Serves 4
1 teaspoon sunflower oil
½ teaspoon ground turmeric
6 green cardamom pods,
　lightly crushed
1 teaspoon coriander seeds,
　lightly crushed
1 garlic clove, crushed
1 cup basmati rice
1²/₃ cups vegetable stock
½ cup plain yogurt
1 tablespoon toasted sunflower seeds
1 tablespoon toasted sesame seeds
salt and freshly ground black pepper
fresh cilantro leaves, to garnish

1 Heat the oil in a non-stick frying pan and fry the spices and garlic for 1 minute, stirring constantly.

2 Add the rice and stock, bring to a boil, then cover and simmer for 15 minutes or until just tender.

3 Stir in the yogurt and the toasted sunflower and sesame seeds. Adjust the seasoning and serve the rice hot, garnished with cilantro leaves.

Indian Pilau Rice

INGREDIENTS

Serves 4

generous 1 cup basmati rice, rinsed
   well
2 tablespoons vegetable oil
1 small onion, finely chopped
1 garlic clove, crushed
1 teaspoon fennel seeds
1 tablespoon sesame seeds
½ teaspoon ground turmeric
1 teaspoon ground cumin
½ teaspoon salt
2 whole cloves
4 green cardamom pods,
   lightly crushed
5 black peppercorns
scant 2 cups vegetable stock
1 tablespoon ground almonds
fresh cilantro sprigs, to garnish

1 Soak the rice in water for 30 minutes. Heat the oil in a saucepan, add the onion and garlic, and fry gently for 5–6 minutes, until softened.

2 Stir in the fennel and sesame seeds, the turmeric, cumin, salt, cloves, cardamom pods and peppercorns and fry for about 1 minute. Drain the rice well, add it to the pan and stir-fry for 3 minutes more.

3 Pour in the vegetable stock. Bring to a boil, then cover, reduce the heat to very low and simmer gently for 20 minutes, without removing the lid, until all the liquid has been absorbed.

4 Remove from the heat and leave to stand for 2–3 minutes. Fluff the rice and stir in the ground almonds. Garnish the rice with cilantro sprigs.

Okra Fried Rice

Sliced okra gives a wonderful creamy texture to this delicious, simple dish.

INGREDIENTS

Serves 3–4

2 tablespoons vegetable oil
1 tablespoon butter or margarine
1 garlic clove, crushed
½ red onion, finely chopped
4 ounces okra, trimmed
2 tablespoons diced green and
   red bell peppers
½ teaspoon dried thyme
2 green chili peppers, finely chopped
½ teaspoon five-spice powder
1 vegetable stock cube
2 tablespoons soy sauce
1 tablespoon chopped fresh cilantro
3 cups cooked rice
salt and freshly ground black pepper
fresh cilantro sprigs, to garnish

1 Heat the oil and butter in a frying pan, add the garlic and onion and cook over medium heat for 5 minutes, until soft.

2 Thinly slice the okra, add to the frying pan and stir-fry gently for 6–7 minutes longer.

3 Add the bell peppers, thyme, chili peppers and five-spice powder and cook for 3 minutes, then crumble in the stock cube.

4 Add the soy sauce, chopped cilantro and rice. Heat through, stirring constantly. Season with salt and pepper. Garnish with cilantro sprigs.

Joloff Rice

This is a good, basic flavored rice that would go with any meat, poultry or fish dish.

INGREDIENTS

Serves 4

2 tablespoons vegetable oil
1 large onion, chopped
2 garlic cloves, crushed
2 tablespoons tomato paste
scant 1³/₄ cups long-grain rice
1 green chili pepper, seeded and
    chopped
pinch of salt
2¹/₂ cups vegetable stock

1 Heat the oil in a large saucepan and fry the onion and garlic for 5 minutes, or until soft. Add the tomato paste and fry over medium heat for about 3 minutes, stirring constantly.

2 Rinse the rice in cold water, drain and add to the pan with the chili and the salt. Continue cooking for 2–3 minutes, stirring all the time to prevent the rice from sticking to the pan.

3 Add the stock, bring to a boil, then cover and simmer over a low heat for about 15 minutes.

4 When the liquid is nearly absorbed, cover the rice with a piece of foil, cover the pan and steam, over low heat, until the rice is thoroughly cooked.

COOK'S TIP

Always wash your hands immediately after seeding and cutting chilies. If you have any cuts on your hands, prevent stinging by wearing rubber gloves while you chop.

Savory Ground Rice

Savory ground rice is served as an accompaniment to soups and stews in West Africa.

INGREDIENTS

Serves 4
1¼ cups milk
1¼ cups water
2 tablespoons butter or margarine
½ teaspoon salt
1 tablespoon chopped fresh parsley
1¼ cups ground rice

1 Place the milk, water and butter or margarine in a saucepan, bring to a boil and add the salt and parsley.

2 Add the ground rice, stirring vigorously with a wooden spoon to prevent the rice from becoming lumpy.

3 Cover the pan and cook over low heat for about 15 minutes, beating the mixture every 2 minutes to prevent lumps from forming.

4 To test if the rice is cooked, rub a pinch of the mixture between your fingers: if it feels smooth and fairly dry, it is ready. Serve hot.

—— COOK'S TIP ——

Ground rice is creamy white and when cooked has a slightly grainy texture. Although often used in sweet dishes, it is a tasty grain to serve with savory dishes too. The addition of milk makes it creamier, but it can be omitted if preferred.

Sweet Rice

In Iran, sweet rice is always served at wedding banquets and on other traditional special occasions.

INGREDIENTS

Serves 8–10

3 oranges
6 tablespoons sugar
3 tablespoons melted butter
5–6 carrots, julienned
½ cup mixed chopped pistachios, almonds and pine nuts
3½ cups basmati rice, soaked in salted water for 2 hours
2–3 saffron strands, soaked in 1 tablespoon boiling water
salt, to taste

1 Cut the peel from the oranges in wide strips using a potato peeler, then cut the peel into thin shreds. Place in a saucepan with enough water to cover and bring to a boil. Simmer for a few minutes, drain and repeat until the peel is no longer bitter.

2 Place the peel back in the pan with 3 tablespoons of the sugar and 4 tablespoons water. Bring to a boil then simmer until the water is reduced by half. Set aside until needed.

3 Heat 1 tablespoon of the butter in a pan and fry the carrots for 2–3 minutes. Add the remaining sugar and 4 tablespoons water and simmer for 10 minutes until almost evaporated.

4 Stir the carrots and half of the nuts into the orange peel and set aside. Drain the rice, boil in salted water for 5 minutes, then reduce the heat and simmer very gently for 10 minutes until half-cooked. Drain and rinse.

5 Heat 1 tablespoon of the remaining butter in the pan, add 3 tablespoons water. Fork a little of the rice into the pan and spoon on some of the carrot mixture. Make layers until all the mixture has been used up.

6 Cook gently for 10 minutes. Pour the remaining butter over all and cover the pan with a clean dish towel. Cover and steam for 30–45 minutes. Serve, garnished with the remaining nuts and the saffron water.

Rice and Fresh Herbs

You can choose your fresh herbs for this dish according to the main course it will accompany.

INGREDIENTS

Serves 4

scant 1½ cups basmati rice, soaked in salt water for 2 hours
2 tablespoons finely chopped fresh parsley
2 tablespoons finely chopped fresh cilantro
2 tablespoons snipped fresh chives
1 tablespoon finely chopped fresh dill
3–4 green onions, finely chopped
4 tablespoons butter
1 teaspoon ground cinnamon
2–3 saffron strands, soaked in 1 tablespoon boiling water
pinch of salt

1 Drain the rice, and then boil in salted water for 5 minutes. Reduce the heat and simmer for 10 minutes.

2 Stir in the parsley, cilantro, chives, dill and green onions and mix well with a fork. Simmer for a few minutes more, then drain but do not rinse. Wash and dry the pan.

3 Heat half of the butter in the pan, add 1 tablespoon water and stir in the rice. Cook over very low heat for 10 minutes, until half-cooked. Add the remaining butter, the cinnamon and saffron water and cover the pan with a clean dish towel. Secure with a tight-fitting lid, and steam over very low heat for 30–40 minutes until tender.

Thai Rice with Bean Sprouts

Thai rice has a delicate fragrance that is delicious hot or cold.

INGREDIENTS

Serves 6

1 cup Thai fragrant rice
2 tablespoons sesame oil
2 tablespoons fresh lime juice
1 small red chili pepper, seeded and chopped
1 garlic clove, crushed
2 teaspoons grated fresh ginger
2 tablespoons light soy sauce
1 teaspoon honey
3 tablespoons pineapple juice
1 tablespoon wine vinegar
2 green onions, sliced
2 canned pineapple rings, chopped
1¼ cups sprouted lentils or beansprouts
1 small red bell pepper, sliced
1 stalk celery, sliced
½ cup cashew nuts, chopped
2 tablespoons toasted sesame seeds
salt and freshly ground black pepper

1 Soak the Thai fragrant rice for 20 minutes, then rinse in several changes of water. Drain, then boil in salted water for 10–12 minutes until tender. Drain and set aside.

2 In a large bowl, whisk together the sesame oil, lime juice, chili, garlic, ginger, soy sauce, honey, pineapple juice and vinegar. Stir in the rice.

3 Add the green onions, pineapple rings, sprouted lentils or beansprouts, red pepper, celery, cashew nuts and the toasted sesame seeds and mix well. If the rice grains stick together while cooling, simply stir them with a metal spoon. This dish can be served warm or lightly chilled and is a good accompaniment to grilled or barbecued meats and fish.

—————— COOK'S TIP ——————

Sesame oil has a strong, nutty flavor and is good for seasoning, marinating or flavoring rather than for cooking. Because the taste is so distinctive, sesame oil can be mixed with grapeseed or other light-flavored oils.

Rice Pilaf

This simple pilaf makes a nice complement to most main course dishes. Alter the dried and fresh herbs to suit your meal.

INGREDIENTS

Serves 6–8
3 tablespoons butter or
    3–4 tablespoons oil
1 onion, finely chopped
generous 2¼ cups long-grain rice
3 cups vegetable stock or water
½ teaspoon dried thyme
1 small bay leaf
salt and freshly ground black pepper
1–2 tablespoons chopped fresh parsley
    or dill or 1–2 tablespoons snipped
    chives, to garnish

1 In a large heavy saucepan, melt the butter or heat the oil over medium heat. Add the onion and cook for 2–3 minutes, until just softened, stirring constantly.

2 Add the rice and cook for about 2 minutes, or until the rice is translucent, stirring frequently. Do not brown.

3 Add the stock or water, dried thyme and bay leaf and season with salt and pepper. Bring to a boil over high heat, stirring frequently. Just as the rice begins to boil, cover the surface with a piece of foil and put the lid on the saucepan. Reduce the heat to very low and cook for 20 minutes (do not lift the cover or stir). Serve hot, garnished with fresh herbs.

----- COOK'S TIP -----

Once cooked, the rice will remain hot for about half an hour, if tightly covered. To reheat the rice, spoon it into a microwave-safe bowl, cover with pierced plastic wrap and microwave on full power for about 5 minutes until hot.

PUDDINGS

Every culture and cuisine seems to have at least one favorite dessert using rice. Even the cold northern Scandinavian countries have a popular winter rice pudding sprinkled liberally with warming cinnamon. In the more exotic climes of Southeast Asia, glutinous sticky rices are simmered with sugar and served with coconut and lemongrass. Short-grain pudding rices, flaked rice and ground rice are the more common favorites, but for an imaginative touch, try using fragrant grains such as basmati or Thai Jasmine in the same way. Rice desserts come in many shapes, too, as they are easy to mold and can be transformed with the addition of whisked egg whites.

Thai Rice Cake

This celebration cake is made from fragrant Thai rice, tangy cream icing and fresh fruit.

INGREDIENTS

Serves 8–10

1 cup Thai fragrant rice
4 cups milk
½ cup sugar
6 green cardamom pods, crushed
2 bay leaves
1¼ cups whipping cream
6 eggs, separated

For the topping

1¼ cups heavy cream
7 ounces sour cream
1 teaspoon vanilla extract
grated rind of 1 lemon
3 tablespoons sugar
berries and sliced star or kiwi fruit, to garnish

1 Grease and line a 9-inch round deep cake pan. Boil the rice in unsalted water for 3 minutes and drain.

2 Return the rice to the pan with the milk, sugar, cardamom and bay leaves. Bring to a boil, then lower the heat and simmer the rice for 20 minutes, stirring occasionally.

3 Allow the mixture to cool, then remove the bay leaves and any cardamom husks. Pour the mixture into a bowl. Beat in the cream and then the egg yolks. Preheat the oven to 350°F.

4 Whisk the egg whites until they form soft peaks, then fold them into the rice mixture. Spoon into the prepared pan and bake for 45–50 minutes until risen and golden brown. The center should be slightly wobbly – it will firm up as the cake cools.

5 Chill the cake overnight in the pan. Turn it out onto a large serving plate. Whip the heavy cream until stiff then gently fold in the sour cream, vanilla extract, lemon rind and sugar.

6 Cover the top and sides of the cake with the cream mixture, swirling it attractively. Garnish with berries and sliced star or kiwi fruit.

Rice Condé Sundae

Cook rice pudding on top of the stove instead of in the oven for a light, creamy texture. It is particularly good served cold topped with fruit, toasted nuts or a trickle of hot chocolate sauce.

INGREDIENTS

Serves 4
generous ¼ cup short-grain
   pudding rice
2½ cups milk
1 teaspoon vanilla extract
½ teaspoon ground cinnamon
3 tablespoons granulated sugar

For the toppings
soft berries such as strawberries,
   raspberries or blueberries
chocolate sauce and flaked toasted
   almonds (optional)

1 Place the rice, milk, vanilla extract, cinnamon and sugar in a saucepan. Bring to a boil, stirring constantly, then reduce the heat to a low simmer.

2 Cook the rice for 30–40 minutes, stirring occasionally. Add some extra milk if it begins to dry out.

3 Make sure the grains are soft, then remove the pan from the heat and allow the rice to cool, stirring it occasionally. When cold, chill the rice pudding in the fridge.

4 Before serving, stir the rice pudding and spoon it into four sundae dishes. Top with fresh fruits, chocolate sauce and almonds, if using.

Ground Rice Pudding

This delicious and light ground rice pudding provides the perfect end to a spicy meal. It can be served hot or cold.

INGREDIENTS

Serves 4–6
¼ cup ground rice
2 tablespoons ground almonds
4 green cardamom pods, crushed
3¾ cups low-fat milk
6 tablespoons sugar
1 tablespoon rosewater

To garnish
1 tablespoon crushed pistachios
edible silver leaf (optional)

1 Place the ground rice and almonds in a saucepan with the cardamom pods. Add 2½ cups of the milk and bring to a boil over medium heat, stirring occasionally.

2 Add the remaining milk and cook over medium heat for about 10 minutes, or until it thickens to the consistency of a creamy soup.

3 Stir in the sugar and rosewater and continue cooking for another 2 minutes. Serve garnished with pistachio nuts and silver leaf, if using.

Orange Rice Pudding

In Spain, Greece, Italy and Morocco, rice puddings are a favorite dish, especially when sweetened with honey and flavored with orange.

INGREDIENTS

Serves 4
4 tablespoons short-grain pudding rice
2½ cups milk
2–3 tablespoons honey
finely grated rind of ½ small orange
⅔ cup heavy cream
1 tablespoon chopped pistachios, toasted

1 Mix the rice with the milk, honey and orange rind in a saucepan.

2 Bring to a boil, then reduce the heat, cover and simmer very gently for about 1¼ hours, stirring regularly.

3 Remove the lid and continue cooking and stirring for about 15–20 minutes, until the rice is creamy.

4 Pour in the cream and simmer for 5–8 minutes longer. Serve the rice sprinkled with the pistachios in individual warmed bowls.

Fruited Rice Ring

This unusual rice pudding looks beautiful turned out of a ring mold, but if you prefer, stir the fruit into the rice and serve in individual dishes.

INGREDIENTS

Serves 4

5 tablespoons short-grain pudding rice
3¾ cups low-fat milk
2½-inch cinnamon stick
1½ cups mixed dried fruit
¾ cup orange juice
3 tablespoons sugar
finely grated rind of 1 small orange

1 Place the rice, milk and cinnamon stick in a large pan and bring to a boil. Cover and simmer, stirring occasionally, for about 1½ hours, until all the liquid has been absorbed.

2 Meanwhile, place the dried fruit and orange juice in a pan and bring to a boil. Cover and simmer very gently for about 1 hour, until the fruit is tender and no liquid remains.

3 Remove the cinnamon stick from the rice and gently stir in the sugar and grated orange rind.

4 Pour the fruit into the base of a lightly oiled 6-cup ring mold. Spoon in the rice, smoothing it down firmly, then chill.

5 Run a knife around the edge of the mold, then carefully turn out the rice ring onto a serving plate.

Yellow Rice Pudding

INGREDIENTS

Serves 6–8

generous 1 cup short-grain pudding
 rice
6¼ cups water
1½ cups sugar
2–3 saffron strands, dissolved in
 1 tablespoon boiling water
4 tablespoons rosewater
½ teaspoon ground cardamom
¼ cup chopped blanched
 almonds
2 tablespoons butter
¼ cup chopped pistachios
1 teaspoon ground cinnamon

1 Preheat the oven to 300°F. Place
 the rice and water in a large pan,
bring to a boil and simmer until the
rice is soft and swollen.

2 Pour 1 cup water into another
 saucepan, add the sugar and simmer
for 10 minutes. Add the saffron,
rosewater, cardamom and half the
almonds. Stir well.

3 Pour the syrup over the rice, add
 the butter and stir well.

4 Pour the rice mixture into an
 ovenproof dish, cover with a lid or
a sheet of aluminum foil and bake for
30 minutes.

5 Remove the pudding from the
 oven and garnish with the
remaining almonds and the pistachios.
Dust with cinnamon and serve warm,
or chill before serving.

Caramel Rice Pudding

This rice pudding is delicious served with crunchy fresh fruit.

INGREDIENTS

Serves 4
4 tablespoons short-grain pudding rice
5 tablespoons raw sugar
pinch of salt
1 can (14 ounces) evaporated milk ,
    plus ³/₄ cup water
knob of butter
1 small fresh pineapple
2 crisp eating apples
2 teaspoons lemon juice

1 Preheat the oven to 300°F. Put the rice in a sieve and wash thoroughly under cold water. Drain well and put into a lightly greased soufflé dish.

2 Add 2 tablespoons sugar and the salt to the dish. Pour on the diluted evaporated milk and stir gently.

3 Dot the surface of the rice with butter and bake for 2 hours, then let cool for 30 minutes.

4 Meanwhile, peel, core and slice the pineapple and apples and then cut the pineapple into chunks. Toss the fruit in lemon juice and set aside.

5 Preheat the broiler and sprinkle the remaining sugar over the rice. Broil for 5 minutes, or until the sugar has caramelized. Let the rice stand for 5 minutes to allow the caramel to harden, then serve with the fresh fruit.

Spiced Rice Pudding

Both Muslim and Hindu communities prepare this pudding, which is traditionally served at mosques and temples.

INGREDIENTS

Serves 4–6
1 tablespoon ghee or melted
    unsalted butter
2-inch cinnamon stick
1 cup light brown sugar
¹/₂ cup ground rice
5 cups milk
1 teaspoon ground cardamom
scant ¹/₂ cup golden raisins
¹/₄ cup slivered almonds
¹/₂ teaspoon grated nutmeg, to serve

1 In a heavy pan, heat the ghee or butter and fry the cinnamon and sugar. Keep frying until the sugar begins to caramelize. Reduce the heat immediately when this happens.

2 Add the rice and half the milk. Bring to a boil, stirring constantly to prevent the milk from boiling over. Reduce the heat and simmer until the rice is cooked, stirring frequently.

3 Add the remaining milk, the cardamom, raisins and almonds and simmer, stirring constantly, to prevent the rice from sticking to the base of the pan. When the mixture has thickened, serve hot or cold, sprinkled with the grated nutmeg.

Black Glutinous Rice Pudding

This unusual rice pudding uses bruised fresh ginger and is quite delicious. Serve in small bowls, with a little coconut cream poured over.

INGREDIENTS

Serves 6
generous ½ cup black glutinous rice
2 cups water
½-inch piece fresh ginger, peeled and bruised
¼ cup dark brown sugar
¼ cup granulated sugar
1¼ cups canned unsweetened coconut milk or cream, to serve

1 Put the rice in a sieve and rinse under cold running water. Drain and put in a large pan with the water. Bring to a boil and stir once to prevent the rice from sticking to the pan. Cover and cook for about 30 minutes.

2 Add the ginger and both the sugars. Cook for another 15 minutes, adding a little more water if necessary, until the rice is thoroughly cooked and creamy.

3 Remove the ginger from the rice and discard it. Serve the pudding warm, in bowls, topping each serving with coconut milk.

—————— COOK'S TIP ——————

For a fresh coconut flavor, choose cartons of coconut cream instead of canned coconut milk. Alternatively, blend a little creamed coconut block with hot water until thick and creamy, then allow to cool before serving.

Souffléed Rice Pudding

Using skim milk to make this pudding is a healthy option, but you can use whole milk if you prefer.

INGREDIENTS

Serves 4

generous ¼ cup short-grain
    pudding rice
3 tablespoons honey
3 cups skim milk
1 vanilla pod or ½ teaspoon
    vanilla extract
2 egg whites
1 teaspoon freshly grated nutmeg

1 Place the rice, honey and milk in a heavy or non-stick saucepan, and bring the milk to a boil, being careful it does not boil over. If using a vanilla pod, add it now.

2 Reduce the heat and cover the pan. Simmer gently for 1-1¼ hours, stirring occasionally to prevent sticking, until most of the liquid has been absorbed.

3 Remove the vanilla pod (rinse and reserve it for another use, if desired), or if using vanilla extract, add it now. Preheat the oven to 425°F.

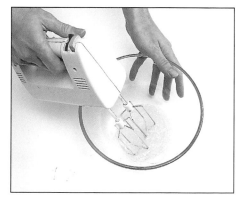

4 Place the egg whites in a large clean, dry bowl and whisk them until they hold in soft peaks.

5 Using either a large metal spoon or spatula, carefully fold the egg whites into the rice and milk mixture. Transfer the pudding to a 4-cup ovenproof dish.

6 Sprinkle with grated nutmeg and bake for 15-20 minutes, until the pudding is well risen and golden brown. Serve hot.

Index